Scottish
Plants
FOR
Scottish
Gardens

Scottish Plants *FOR* *Scottish* Gardens

Jill, Duchess of Hamilton
and
Dr Franklyn Perring

ROYAL
BOTANIC
GARDEN
EDINBURGH

Edited by Norma M Gregory

MERCAT PRESS: EDINBURGH

First Published 1996 by The Stationery Office Limited
Reprinted 1997 by The Stationery Office Limited
Reprinted 2000 by Mercat Press
53 South Bridge, Edinburgh EH1 1YS

ISBN 1873644 892

Designed by Derek Munn MCSD, The Stationery Office Graphic Design
Illustrations by Steve Earl

Acknowledgements

I am extremely grateful to the many people who have contributed to this book. Space does not allow me to name them all but I must first acknowledge a great debt of gratitude to my co-author Franklyn Perring, and to Richard Pankhurst and Chris Preston who compiled the checklist of Scottish native plants on which this book is founded. Norma Gregory, my collaborator at the Royal Botanic Garden Edinburgh, has ably edited the book and her colleague, Douglas McKean, must be acknowledged for the vital job of authenticating all of the photographs used. A book on the Scottish flora would be a poor thing without recognition of our Gaelic heritage and I must thank Joan Clark and Mary Beith for their advice in this area, as well as Professor Ian MacDonald for providing the Gaelic plant names. However, I could never have succeeded in pulling all these strands together without the support of my associate at Flora for Fauna, Penny Hart. I must also convey my gratitude to the following for their advice, technical expertise and support: Alan Bennell, Hugh Cheape, Gina Douglas, Iseabail Macleod, John Marsden, the Hon. Miriam Rothschild, Liz Sellen, Maureen Sherriff, Bill Smith, Clive Stace, and Stephen Wood, but especially to the Botanical Society of the British Isles whose database of British native plants was the primary source for our Scottish checklist. The idea for the book evolved from the Flora for Fauna Indigenous Plant Garden at the Royal Highland Show in 1995. The sponsors of the Garden, Matthew Gloag & Son and Scottish Natural Heritage, must therefore be acknowledged as progenitors of this book. I especially thank Roderick James and his firm Carpenter Oak and Woodland for building the oak arbour for the launch of this book at the Chelsea Flower Show. I also thank our other sponsors, especially RTZ-CRA, Osbourne and Little and Kleinwort Benson. Finally, I must thank my former husband, the Duke of Hamilton, for reintroducing me to Scotland and its wonderful flora and fauna.

Photo credits

With the exception of those listed below, all photographs used in this book were taken from the Royal Botanic Garden Edinburgh's slide collection.
Brinsley Burbidge: cover photo; Andrew M Gagg, Photoflora: *Prunus avium, Salix pentandra, S. viminalis, Campanula rotundifolia, Lathyrus linifolius, Pilosella officinarum, Scutellaria galericulata, Veronica officinalis;* Franklyn Perring: *Alnus glutinosa, Betula pubescens, Taxus baccata, Ulex gallii, Allium ursinum, Campanula latifolia, Helianthemum nummularium, Hypericum androsaemum, Leucanthemum vulgare, Lysimachia vulgaris, Ranunculus una, Silene uniflora;* William Tait: *Ilex aquifolium, Pinus sylvestris, Primula scotica.*

Research and illustrations supported by

Shell U.K. Limited

Printed in Hong Kong through World Print Ltd

CONTENTS

FOREWORD

By Magnus Magnusson KBE

Scottish Plants for Scottish Gardens is a book which is long overdue. It is intriguing, helpful, and utterly compelling. It challenges us to deal with the vital question of preserving plants which are native to Scotland – and, in some cases, reintroducing them.

Our forefathers had an intimate knowledge of our plant life: which ones were suitable for making dyes, which ones had healing properties, which ones were good for eating. But how many of us really know which plants are indigenous to Scotland and are therefore part of our natural heritage? It is a sad fact of life that we have lost so much of this knowledge and experience.

Jill, Duchess of Hamilton, has served us all well by bringing to our attention the imperative need to revive this knowledge and preserve these plants. From the majestic Caledonian pine to the tiny, fragile Scottish primrose (*Primula Scotica*), we have a living wealth of history and tradition. How fascinating it is to read the story of our well-known and well-loved trees and shrubs like the silver birch and the heather – and then to learn about the less-known Scots lovage and where to find it round the coasts of Scotland.

We are all gardeners at heart. Knowledge brings enjoyment – so next time you go for a walk, take this book with you; it will add enormously to the pleasure of your outing. And when you come home, have a look at your own garden and see how you can help to preserve some of these plants by planting them at home, wherever practical.

As Chairman of Scottish Natural Heritage I am delighted to see this timely focus on Scotland's indigenous plants (after all, it is more than 150 years since anyone has written on this subject). I hope that the knowledgeable enthusiasm which illuminates this book will inspire us all to cultivate and grow as many of them as possible in our gardens. We all have a positive part to play to maintain and enhance the rich biodiversity of the flora and fauna to be found and fostered right on our own doorsteps.

Magnus Magnusson

Introduction

Jill, Duchess of Hamilton

INTRODUCTION

*Through fields where the ghosts
Of the marsh and the moorland
Still ride the old marches`
Despising the plough.*

*The marsh and the moorland
Are not to be banished;
The bracken and heather,
The glory of broom,
Usurp all the balks
And the fields' broken fringes,
And claim from the sower
Their portion of room ...*

'SCOTLAND' Sir Alexander Gray (1882–1968)

LIKE ALL NATIONS WITH AN ANCIENT CULTURE, SCOTLAND HAS A STRONG RURAL tradition, based on an intimate knowledge of the native vegetation. The cereal crops which were the staple food may be ancient imports, but virtually every facet of life depended on, or was influenced by, the native flora. The Scot needed oaks to tan his leather, flowers for the sweetness of honey, and herbs for his medicines. Even that most famous of Scots traditions, tartan cloth, owed its colours to dyes derived from plants. Despite their rumbustious reputation, the clans prized the graceful forms and subtle colours of their local flora. So much so that many chose those plants for their clan badge: the MacDonalds wore a bunch of heather; the MacIntoshes, a holly branch; the Grants, Scots pine. The Country's most enduring symbol, the thistle, was the badge of the ruling Stewarts. Scottish place names are often witness to the importance of local plants, Blanerne for example, which is from the Gaelic for 'alder sted', or Cowden meaning 'hazel knolls', acknowledgement, perhaps, of the trees that gave shelter and warmth to the early inhabitants. Sixteen of the eighteen letters of the Gaelic alphabet correspond to an indigenous tree or shrub.

Now much of the flora that underpins Scottish place names, poetry and heritage is threatened by farming, forestry and spread of towns. The Highlands and Islands are still among the great wildlife areas of the world, but despite the preservation of selected parts of a priceless natural landscape, Scotland has lost a huge proportion of its plant heritage. The majority of trees in Scotland are now conifers of foreign origin. Of the tens of thousands of square miles originally covered with Scots pine little more than forty-two square miles remain. There is however, a new determination to resist the spread of alien vegetation and return parts of Scotland to a more historically natural state. Plants which are both indigenous to Scotland and local to each area can then be restored to their rightful role as the backbone of the Scottish landscape. Every Scot can help in this. By choosing to grow local plants, whether it be in a window box or in the formal grounds of a stately home; in public parks or car parks; in agricultural set-aside and on roadside verges; on golf course roughs or in the thousands of gardens that surround people's homes in cities and villages. But what is Scotland's native flora? And what makes it unique?

Before the seas rose and cut off what is now the British Isles, Scotland was part of the fringe of continental Europe. But since the separation some 10,000 years ago, the British flora, although similar to its continental neighbour, has developed distinctive differences.

Even though most Scottish plants are either European species or close relatives, they have evolved to suit local conditions, so even those which are the same genus and species, in fact, can vary minutely in appearance or chemical composition in different areas. Hawthorn from Hungary, for example, has fewer thorns than Scottish hawthorn. Local adaptation has not only made Scottish plants better fitted to local soil and climate, but also it has ensured that they are uniquely suited to the variety of indigenous animals whose survival depends on them.

There are over twenty species of plants which are endemic to Scotland – that is plants which are not found anywhere else in the world – of which *Primula scotica* is the most famous. Primulas, which are grouped loosely under the three main headings of primroses, cowslips and primulas, are found all over the world, but *Primula scotica* grows naturally only in Scotland. Perhaps the most distinctly 'Scottish' plants are the Highland alpines which are not native to any other part of the British Isles.

Over seventy plant species in Scotland do not occur in England. Fifty others are so much more numerous in Scotland than in their confined corners of England and Wales that they can be regarded as characteristic of Scotland. In addition to these, there are over a hundred predominantly Scottish plants in the north of the country which become rare towards the south. Scurvygrass *(Cochlearia officinalis)* grows on the most northerly tip of Scotland and is found round the coasts of the British Isles. Scots lovage *(Ligusticum scoticum)*, a member of the parsley family, is confined to the Scottish and Northern Irish coasts, apart from a few sites in Northumberland. Some of Scotland's most prized natives are small, such as dwarf birch *(Betula nana)*, dwarf willow *(Salix herbacea)*, oyster plant *(Mertensia maritima)*, alpine lady's-mantle *(Alchemilla alpina)*, Scottish primrose *(Primula scotica)*, and spring squill *(Scilla verna)*. Distinguishing native from non-native flora is made more difficult because along with the familiar native plants – foxgloves, violets, hawthorn, oak, ivy, honeysuckle, and oxeye daisies – there are some non-natives from England which became well established even before the introduction of alien plants from overseas. Most prominent among these in Scotland is the beech.

Small variations in appearance occasionally mean that a plant is classified separately, sometimes as a variety or subspecies. The Scots pine *(Pinus sylvestris)*, which grows in all the northern regions of Europe, Asia and North America, is an example. The Caledonian pine of Scotland has slight genetic differences from the Scots pine which so freely colonised the heaths of Surrey and Dorset.

It has never been easy for the general public to find out which plants are native to Scotland. Although flora and fauna were an integral part of Gaelic poetry, there was no formal book on the subject in Scotland until Sir Robert Sibbald's *Prodromus Historiae Naturalis Scotica*, which was written in Latin and published in 1684 and 1696. The next Scottish Flora was John Lightfoot's *Flora Scotica* published in

1777, which gives economic uses of plants, and includes the first written record in English of a selection of dyes. Since Sir William Hooker's *Flora Scotica* of 1841 (which is now outdated, and scarce), no comprehensive book has been published on Scotland's native flora.

Various county and island Floras in Scotland have been published this century, usually as reference books for specialists and are now seldom available. Excellent though these may have been – or are – they do not cover all the counties. To discover if a plant is native a Scot has to refer to one of the books on the flora of the entire British Isles. Space restrictions mean that most entries fail to give detailed plant localities. Only the *Atlas of the British Flora* (edited by F. H. Perring and S. M. Walters and published in 1962) gives distribution maps of the flora of Scotland, and Ireland also has an up to date published flora.

To help remedy the shortage of information and to assist the non-specialist in distinguishing between native or alien plants, this book introduces a *Check-list of Scotland's Native Flora* comprising the 1,085 indigenous ferns and flowering plants – compiled by Richard Pankhurst of the Royal Botanic Garden Edinburgh and Chris Preston of the Biological Records Centre at Monks Wood Experimental Station. Plant names are given in Latin, English, Gaelic and Scots.

The plants in this list are our plant heritage. Robert the Bruce never saw a rhododendron. Nor did Robert Burns. It is unlikely that either of them ever saw a petunia, a fuschia, a dahlia, or a zinnia. The number of plants in the Scottish landscape and in Scottish gardens was then very limited. The favoured exotic was still the red rose celebrated in Burns' well-known poem.

In the 1800s, plant hunters returning from the Himalayas provided hundreds of species of rhododendrons which, like their native relatives the heathers, have rooted so permanently into the landscape that there is now sometimes a mistaken belief that they are Scottish. The passion for conifers displayed by Queen Victoria and Prince Albert set the trend for the introduction of trees such as *Wellingtonia*, monkey-puzzle, Douglas fir, Japanese cedar, Sitka spruce and Monterey cypress. Such was the influx of new species that native plants were often displaced from gardens.

So great has been the impact of alien plants on vegetation that much of the Scottish flora has been dismissed as 'wildflowers', worthy only of untamed places such as hedgerows or roadside verges. Yet many of the most familiar plants in these habitats are, in fact, imports and escapees from gardens. The wallflower, for instance, profuse around the Castle Rock, Edinburgh, and on railway embankments, originates in the Mediterranean region. This, and thousands of other plants, arrived on the soles of Roman sandals or they escaped from gardens, or the seeds were dispersed by birds and winds, or they infiltrated over the centuries in sacks of cereal seeds. Some foreign plants from as far off as Asia Minor arrived in Scotland in this way. Others were later imported with sand, gravel and cinders used to build railway embankments and canal banks. Consequently, it is difficult to find out when a plant was first discovered, and whether or not it is native.

Well over 40,000 varieties of exotic plants are available to Scots gardeners, most of whom now grow mixtures of native, introduced and highly hybridised plants. Although many introductions – accidental or deliberate – add beauty to the countryside, it has usually been at the expense of native species. Of the 60 or so conifers grown, only three are indigenous.

Among the many private gardens and estates open to the public, none has ever been advertised as containing only indigenous plants. The lack of cultivated native plants did not matter when there was an abundant natural habitat, but since the destruction of so much wild countryside by industrialisation, agriculture and housing, gardens are becoming an important haven for indigenous species. Using native plants can give gardens a distinctive quality and preserve regional identity.

Scottish native plants have many advantages for the gardener. They are well suited to the harsh and unpredictable climate and often seed prolifically, which cannot be said for many introduced species. Nevertheless, it would be wrong to think that there are no problems. Many of our native plants are under threat precisely because they require specialised habitats, and the rich soils of gardens and heavy competition from more aggressive plants mean that cultivation of some of the shy or more interesting wild plants needs some care and adjustment of growing conditions. The species covered in this book, however, should be suited to most Scottish gardens with either neutral or acid soils. They have been selected for their attractiveness in flower, fruit or foliage and are suitable for a range of garden habitats – shade, rock garden, herbaceous border, ponds and pond margins. Those species, such as lesser celandine, which can create problems by becoming too aggressive, have been excluded. Most of the plants listed should be available from nurseries.

There is a wider perspective to the encouragement of a native flora than just the plants themselves or our enjoyment of them. Many native animals are highly selective in their nutritional requirements and will feed and reproduce only on specific local plants. The panda's dependence on bamboo is well known but there are many examples closer to home such as the caterpillar of the small tortoiseshell butterfly which will eat only stinging nettles. Thousands of insect species rely solely on one or two specific plants either for nourishment or for egg-laying. If these are absent the insects die out.

More than seventy percent of Scottish birds are insectivorous, so without plants which support insects, birds weaken and starve. Anything which supports a rich insect life, whether silver birch, hawthorn, leaf litter, an old decaying log or compost heap, can be a natural larder for birds, hedgehogs, bats and other animals. The introduced horse-chestnut tree supports only four insect species in Scotland, whereas the native hawthorn supports over 220. In contrast, in its native lands, Albania and Greece, the horse-chestnut will host a wide variety of insect life. Many gardeners unwittingly condemn plants to celibacy by not having the right balance to encourage pollinating insects. Although more than half of Scottish plants are self or wind-pollinated, a very large number, especially those grown in gardens, depend on a vast range of insect pollination. Failing this, they fail to set fruit. Sadly, in the last decade there has been a sharp decline in numbers of one of the main pollinators, bumble-bees, because of the decrease in nectar-rich plants.

Promoting Scottish plants is more than flag-waving patriotism. In their natural habitat native plants are the basis of all life. They feed and protect the insects and lower life forms which in turn sustain birds and small creatures which then provide food for the larger carnivores. Over thousands of years, Scottish animals have co-evolved with the Scottish flora, and in the process, the animals have come to favour certain plants, even depend on them. The plants – and the micro-organisms and invertebrates which they support – are the keys to flourishing life cycles and the maintenance of biodiversity.

Biodiversity is more than an abstract concept – there are very practical advantages. The encouragement of pollinators is one already referred to, but another is natural control of pests. Many gardeners fear that, unless deterred, insects will become pests and devour their plants. Gardens which include a rich selection of regional native plants enable carnivores – predators of pests such as aphids and snails – to breed and feed. As most of the country's wildlife lives on privately owned land, it is essential that landowners grow regional plants. In this way they and all who garden can play an important part in building a flourishing wildlife mosaic.

The
Plants

Franklyn Perring

TREES AND SHRUBS

Alnus glutinosa alder

One of our commonest deciduous, waterside trees rarely exceeding 15m. Recognised by its black fissured bark and the broad, unpointed, rich-green leaves. The reddish flowers are borne on separate male and female catkins in clusters of two to six at the end of branches. The females are small, up to 5mm, bud-like, the males are drooping up to 30mm. The flowers open in March and, after pollination, the females develop into cones, at first green but later black which shed seed in the autumn but then persist for several years.

Alder is found throughout Scotland, except the northern isles, where the water-table is constantly high on stream and loch sides and in marsh-land from sea-level to 500m. It grows best where the pH is over 6.0.

With attractive leaves and spring catkins it is a suitable small tree for a large garden with a stream or waterlogged area. Easily raised from seed sown in spring on any seed compost. Can be planted out any time from October to March. Very tolerant of cutting so may be coppiced if it grows too large.

Alders attract siskins which feed on the seeds in winter, and are host to over 90 species of insect including three kinds of gall-mite.

Betula pendula silver birch

A common pioneer, deciduous tree of dry soils which may reach 30m in 50 to 60 years. When young it has shiny reddish-brown bark and erect branches but, with age, the bark becomes silver and the shoots droop so justifying both English and Latin names. The slender, juvenile branches are covered in tiny warts but are otherwise hairless. Leaves unfold in May and develop into a triangular wedge shape with a double-toothed margin. Male and female catkins occur – the male appear in autumn but only release the wind-blown pollen when the females emerge and ripen with the leaves.

Silver birch grows up to 750m throughout Scotland, except the northern isles, and prefers dry acid soils in the open, unshaded by other trees.

The beautiful bark, pendulous branches and catkins combined with quick growth make

this an ideal garden tree giving pleasure throughout the year. Easily raised from seed which can be sown as soon as it ripens in autumn: plant out in its second winter.

One of the most valuable trees for wildlife supporting 230 species of insects including buff tip moths and sawflies. The caterpillars of these in summer and the seeds in autumn attract tits, goldfinches, siskins and redpolls.

Betula pubescens downy birch

Similar to silver birch but usually only reaching 25m at maturity and lacking the long pendulous branches of that species. The bark becomes silver or greyish-white but lacks the black diamond-shaped patches which are often a feature of silver birch trunks. However, more easily distinguished from that species by the young twigs being softly hairy,

not warted, and by the leaves being rounded in outline, not triangular, and having single rather than double teeth at the margin.

Downy birch thrives on acid soils up to 750m throughout Scotland but prefers much damper sites than silver birch such as bogs, fens and loch margins: it is thus suited to the higher rainfall areas of the country.

A valuable tree for planting in exposed, upland gardens. Here subsp. *tortuosa* may be used – this is a multi-stemmed, more shrubby form adapted to severe growing conditions.

Like the silver birch, *B. pubescens* is host to many insects including two species of tortricoid moths. Old trees often develop 'Witches-brooms', caused by a gall-forming fungus, which may be taken over by birds as nesting sites.

Calluna vulgaris heather

This low-growing evergreen rising to about 60cm is our commonest mountain and moorland shrub with prostrate or ascending, twiggy much-branched stems. The branches have closely-packed, scale-like leaves, 1–2mm long, arranged in opposite pairs. The bell-shaped flowers, which first appear in mid-summer, arise singly in the leaf axils, each with 4-lobed, pinkish-purple sepals hiding the petals: they develop dry, round capsules with few dust-like seeds.

Heather only thrives where the soil is acid with a pH below 6.5, but ranges from dry heath to the wettest of bogs from sea-level to over 700m throughout Scotland.

Dozens of different varieties of heather, with a wide selection of colours to choose from, are cultivated and available from nurseries although 'Lucky' white heather is still to be found in the wild. The wild form can be raised from seed collected in October to November, dried and sieved, and sown in spring on a peat substitute/sand mixture in a cold frame. Though tolerant of shade, heather flowers most freely in full sun.

The low-growing mounds of mature plants protect ground-feeding birds like wrens in winter whilst the nectar-filled flowers attract bees – but beware of some cultivars which are sterile.

Corylus avellana hazel

A small deciduous tree up to 10m but more usually maintained as a multi-stemmed shrub of 3–5m by regular coppicing on a seven to

14 year cycle. The alternate leaves are round with drawn-out tips, hairs on both surfaces and saw-tooth edges. Identified in winter by small grey, male catkins which expand in February into the familiar 'lambs'-tails' –

clusters of flowers shedding copious pollen. Female catkins, looking like large leaf buds with protruding red tassels, develop at the same time ripening into clusters of two to three 'cob nuts' by autumn.

Hazel is common on a wide range of soils and is one of the few taller-growing woody plants which tolerates extreme conditions in Scotland forming 'woodland' in the Outer Hebrides and ascending to 650m in Atholl.

Because its size can be regulated by coppicing and it is most attractive when full of catkins in winter or with yellow leaves in autumn, this is an ideal shrub for the small garden. Easily raised from 'nuts' sown 5-7cm apart – but they will need protection from mice and squirrels!

Whilst the pollen attracts many early foraging bees the plant is also host to 70 other insect species including the long-snouted nut weevil.

Crataegus monogyna hawthorn

The commonest constituent of our hedgerows because, with clipping and laying, hawthorn can become a thorny, impenetrable barrier to stock and neighbouring dogs. It will also grow into a handsome small tree up to 15m if left uncut. The bark on old trunks is greyish-brown with many small scales. The leaves are divided into five to seven lobes, largest at the base, reaching almost to the mid-vein. The showy, 5-petalled, white flowers, often pink in bud, occur in masses which are strongly and sweetly scented and develop into an almost never-failing crop of single-seeded 'haws' which persist throughout the winter.

Hawthorn grows on all but the poorest soils up to about 500m and is a pioneer, forming dense scrub which does not survive in heavy shade.

With its masses of flowers in May and June and colourful winter berries, hawthorn makes a splendid shrub for gardens of all sizes and can be controlled by regular pruning. Easily raised from cuttings, or from seed gathered in October and sown in a peat substitute/sand mixture: but beware, most take 18 months to germinate.

One of the most important shrubs for wildlife, providing food for 150 insect species, including yellow-tail moth, hawthorn shield-bug and many nectar-feeding flies. In hard winters it feeds many visiting redwings and fieldfares.

Cytisus scoparius broom

A wiry, erect shrub up to 2m with hairless, 5-angled, green stems which bear short-lived leaves – the lower with three and the upper reduced to one, leaflet. In May and June it produces a mass of bright golden, pea-like flowers, each about 2cm long on slender

stalks. These develop pods in September which are explosive – the two halves coiling up after splitting.

Broom is widespread on light, sandy, acid heaths and woodland margins throughout Scotland except the northern isles, reaching 650m in Atholl.

Its masses of spring flowers and unaggressive habit make this an essential shrub for dry sandy soils, especially for small gardens, where it will thrive best in full sunshine. Can be raised from seed: however germination may be erratic and, as the plants do not transplant easily, it is best to sow a few seeds together in containers and thin out all but the strongest.

Although broom does not produce nectar, the flowers have a trigger mechanism which sprays pollen onto visiting bees. The leaves are fed on by green hairstreak caterpillars whilst the pods are host to a two-winged gall-midge.

Erica cinerea **bell heather**

A small evergreen shrub with numerous branched stems and very small, shiny, dark-green leaves arranged in whorls of three, with turned-back margins which hide the under-surface. The reddish-purple, bell-shaped flowers are borne in dense terminal spikes and appear in July. The tiny seed capsules, which ripen in autumn, are inside the persistent dead flowers.

Bell heather thrives only on acid soils with pH below 6.5 and is found on moors and heaths throughout Scotland and up to 1,200m in Inverness-shire.

With its tight, neat habit and long flowering season it is a good plant for a dry sunny part of an acid garden. It is easily propagated from cuttings taken in late summer from the present year's growth. Many different colour forms may be available from local nurseries.

The low-growing mounds protect ground-feeding birds such as wrens and are less prone to grazing by rabbits than common heather. Nectar-filled flowers attract solitary wasps but if the flowers are too narrow for their heads they bore in from the side and by-pass the pollination mechanism. It is the food plant of true lover's knot, one of our commonest moorland moths.

Hedera helix **ivy**

An unmistakable woody-stemmed climber which can reach 30m up rocks and trees holding on only by little rootlets produced along its stems. It is not a parasite and gains neither food nor water from the plants it clings to. Without support ivy grows well along the ground. Its leaves vary in shape: the lower are triangular and 3–5- lobed whilst those at the top and on flowering shoots may be oval and uncut. Clusters of 5-petalled, greenish-yellow flowers appear in autumn which develop into round, black berries.

Ivy grows throughout most of lowland Scotland up to about 500m on all but the most acid and wet soils, usually in woodland and other sheltered situations although it may be cut back by severe frosts if unprotected.

A very useful plant for gardens, giving excellent ground cover in shady areas where little else will grow and is toleratant of atmospheric pollution. It is most easily raised from cuttings taken in late summer and there are many different leaf forms to choose from. This is a plant which is wonderful for wildlife! The dense cover that ivy creates on trees and walls is an invaluable habitat for nests in summer and sheltering birds in winter. The nectar-filled flowers are fed on by wasps and flies by day and by moths by night including Green-bridled Crescent and Swordgrass. In spring the fruits are relished by thrushes and blackbirds.

Ilex aquifolium holly

One of our few evergreen, broad-leaved shrubs, unmistakeable because of its glossy, dark-green leaves which are generally very prickly on young plants but often have a smooth edge on old specimens or in the upper part. The clustered, fragrant white flowers have four petals: there are separate males and females – usually on separate trees. Holly grows on a wide range of soils throughout most of lowland Scotland ascending to 550m in Argyll, but it is absent from much of the north and east as it does not produce mature berries where the July minimum is below 12°C.

Invaluable for gardens both for hedges, which are effective wind-breaks throughout the year, and also as individual specimens, where one of the variegated cultivars may be preferred. Berry-producing females are attractive, but one male is needed for every six females to ensure pollination. To obtain such a ratio, cuttings may be safer than raising plants from seed, especially as the latter take 18 to 20 months to germinate.

As well as giving cover and shelter to small birds in all seasons, holly produces welcome berries for redwings, fieldfares and mistle thrushes in winter. Caterpillars of two tortricoid moths feed on the leaves which are often also attacked by a leaf-miner.

Juniperus communis juniper

The smallest of our three native conifers and the most useful in smaller gardens. Recognised by its short, spine-tipped leaves, 8–20mm long but only c.1mm wide, blue–green above with a silver line below. There are separate male and female bushes: the cones which develop on the latter ripen in two to three years and become bluish-black.
There are two forms: the upright subsp. *communis*, which reaches 3m, is native in the south and east of Scotland whilst the prostrate subsp. *alpina* is the common form

Its dark-green, oval leaves are arranged in opposite pairs. The familiar flowers are 2.5cm long with a two-lipped mouth: they are purplish-red outside and pale yellow within and develop into red berries.

Honeysuckle grows on a wide range of soils in hedgerows, woodlands and on cliffs throughout Scotland reaching 500m in Atholl.

As one of the most beautiful and fragrant of our flowering shrubs, which can be incorporated into a hedge or trained up a trellis, it is a native no garden should be without, especially as it has two flowering periods – early summer and September. Easily raised from late summer cuttings which can be planted out 12 months later in clusters of two or three together.

The scent, which is strongest in the evening, and the nectar at the bottom of the tube, attract pollinating moths whilst the red berries are food for blackcaps, blackbirds, robins, thrushes and tits. The dense tangled stems make excellent nest sites.

in the north and west. Both ascend to about 900m and thrive on basic as well as acid soils so long as they are free-draining.

Both forms are useful garden shrubs but subsp. *alpina* is especially valuable as ground cover in open exposed situations. It is easily propagated from cuttings of the present year's wood in late summer or early autumn: it is much more difficult from seed.

The shoot tips are infected by gall-midges which produce a 'whooping gall' once used medicinally in the treatment of whooping cough. The berries are attractive to birds: they swallow them whole and then drop the hard black seeds. The bushes also provide year-round cover for thrushes and goldcrests.

Lonicera periclymenum honeysuckle

A deciduous climber which supports itself by twining its woody stems round other shrubs or the branches of trees, climbing up to 6m.

Pinus sylvestris Scots pine

A conifer with reddish-brown bark which may grow to 35m. The blue-green needles are in pairs and only 5–7cm long. The female flowers, like miniature red cones, receive golden, wind-blown pollen from catkin-like clusters of male flowers and develop woody cones up to 8cm with the lower scales turned down at maturity.

Prunus avium **wild cherry or gean**

This handsome deciduous tree rises to 25m and may be recognised by its shining reddish-brown bark with the horizontal stripes which are characteristic of cherries in general The leaves are elliptical, saw-edged and softly hairy beneath. The beautiful clusters of cup-shaped, 5-petalled, white flowers burst before the leaves open in late April or early May. These develop into blackish-red, usually sour 'cherries' by July, so long as there are two or more trees as they are self-sterile.

Scots pine is a true native in the Highlands of Scotland ascending to 700m and often the dominant tree in the Caledonian Forest. However it is also widely naturalised and can be grown on most soils with a pH below 6.5 whether free-draining or waterlogged.

The true patriot will surely wish to plant one of these splendid trees though they are best suited to the larger garden. They can only be propagated by sowing seed collected from fully ripe cones, preferably of native origin, raised in nursery beds for two years (thinning as necessary) and then planted in the permanent site.

The seeds are the main food of crossbills and, if the cone crop fails, the birds leave the area. The needles are food for the caterpillars of many moths, including the pine beauty and the pine looper, which in turn are food for tits and other insectivores.

A species of lowland woods on fertile soils throughout Scotland except the north and west and the outer isles. Often in the understorey layer of oak woods.

One of our most attractive, native woodland trees suitable for gardens of all sizes where it will tolerate light shade. It is easily propagated from seed gathered at the same time as the birds move in and stored, with the 'pulp' removed, until the following spring when it can be sown in nursery beds. Thin as necessary and plant when four to five years old.

17

Larger species of birds such as starlings and pigeons enjoy the fruit but it is too big for small birds. The leaves are eaten by forest bugs, one of our largest shieldbugs, and by the caterpillars of several species of moths. The leaves are galled by the same fungus which causes peach-leaf curl.

Prunus padus bird cherry

A shrub or small tree growing up to 15m tall with a strong-smelling, brown bark. The elliptical, light-green leaves have prominent veins and a neatly toothed margin. The almond-scented white flowers, which grow in

drooping sprays of up to 40 to a stalk, appear in late May after the leaves have unfolded. They develop into bitter-tasting, black berries which ripen in July.

Bird cherry is found on acid soils in moist, deciduous oak and birch woodlands and scrub throughout lowland Scotland but reaches 400m in Rannoch: it is absent from the outer isles.

Invaluable for gardens of all sizes with its most attractive flowers, and leaves which turn through yellow to red before falling in October. Easily propagated from fruits collected in July and stored, with the 'pulp' removed, until the following spring. It can then be sown, thinned and planted out in the same way as wild cherry.

The flowers attract many pollinating bees or flies. The fruit, like small cherries, are full of

tannin and inedible to humans but, as the name implies, are enjoyed by birds and, as they are smaller than wild cherries, can be swallowed by robins and thrushes.

Known locally as 'hag cherry' or 'hag berry' from the tree's old Norse name *heggr*.

Prunus spinosa blackthorn or sloe

A thorny, deciduous, branched shrub up to 4m often suckering to form dense thickets. The elliptic leaves are finely toothed and hairy beneath. The masses of small, pure-white flowers appear before the leaves in March and April and ripen by September/October into the familiar round, blue-black 'sloes' of hedgerows.

Blackthorn is widespread in the lowlands of

Scotland but ascends to 400m. Apart from hedges, where it is often planted, it grows wild on cliffs, in scrub and on woodland margins on all types of soils except the most acid.

Useful as a hedging plant in gardens, especially in exposed positions and attractive both for its early flowering and for the fruits which can be used to prepare 'sloe' gin once frost has reduced the tannin content. Easily propagated from seed which can be treated in the same way as wild cherry: seedlings can be planted out after three years.

The dense cover and sharp thorns of a blackthorn hedge make excellent, well-protected nesting sites for garden birds whilst

the flowers produce nectar for humble bees and early-flying small tortoiseshells. The leaves are host to a gall-midge which may produce 60 'blisters' round the margin of a single leaf.

Sometimes known as 'bullister' from the Gaelic *buileastair*.

Salix caprea goat willow

A deciduous shrub or small tree which can reach 10m, with a short trunk and pleasing, rounded outline. The leaves too are rounded, green above but white and woolly beneath. There are separate male and female plants: the former produce the golden-yellow, round, fluffy catkins which are often called 'pussy willows'. The female catkins are longer, greener and much less attractive. A mountain form, var. *sphacelata*, is a gnarled shrub with densely-hairy young leaves.

Goat willow is native in oak woods, montane scrub and in hedges, mainly on basic soils, throughout Scotland, though rare in the outer isles and ascending to 825m (as var. *sphacelata*).

The male, with its wonderful catkins in March and April before the leaves, makes a

splendid garden plant, growing best in a sunny position: it does not require the damp conditions needed by other willows. Plants are best raised from hardwood cuttings so that the males can be selected. In any case growing willows from seed is often difficult.

Second in importance only to oak as a species for wildlife, providing food for over 200 different insects. The male catkins are full of nectar and pollen for bees whilst the leaves feed the caterpillars of the sallow kitten, common quaker and puss moth. Tits soon find them.

Salix lapponum downy willow

A low-growing deciduous shrub up to 1m, occasionally more, with stems at first woolly but becoming glossy with age. The oval or rounded leaves are silvery-grey and downy, often with a twisted tip. The male and female catkins, on separate plants, are yellowish-grey and upright, up to 4cm long and open in May and June: the males have yellow anthers whilst the females have a slender conspicuous style, and grow to c.7cm after fertilisation.

Downy willow is locally common on cliffs and rocky slopes throughout the Highlands at altitudes between 200 and 900m.

The woolly leaves make this an attractive willow for the rock garden, the male especially so with its colourful upright catkins. The var. *stuartii*, which comes from Perthshire, may be preferred as it is also conspicuous in winter with yellow shoots and orange buds. Like other willows this is easily raised from hardwood cuttings taken in the autumn.

The pollen and/or nectar in the male and female catkins provide food for bumble-bees,

bee-flies and solitary wasps attracted by a certain sallow-like scent. The leaves can be host to the larvae of sawflies and a number of noctuid and tortricoid moths.

Salix pentandra bay willow

A large deciduous shrub or small tree up to about 15m with twigs shining as if varnished. The mainly elliptical leaves are also shining – glossy-green above but distinctly paler beneath: the margins are finely and regularly toothed. Catkins appear with the leaves in late May or June: the males are a beautiful golden-yellow 2–5cm long, the females are green and shorter and do not release their seeds until winter.

Bay willow is frequent by streams and in wet ground, including sand dunes, in south and east Scotland ascending to about 400m.

A valuable small tree for gardens because of its attractive foliage and catkins (particularly the male) which thrives well outside its native range. Called 'Bay' because of its resemblance to the true bay, *Laurus nobilis*, not only because of the shape and colour of the leaves but also because they emit a pleasant aroma when unfolding or if crushed. Best propagated, like other willows, by taking hardwood cuttings in autumn.

The catkins provide pollen and/or nectar for many species of wild bees and wasps attracted by the aromatic scent, whilst the leaves are host to the caterpillars of several species of moth.

Salix viminalis osier

An erect deciduous shrub 3–5m tall with long, slender, flexible branches and delicate, narrow, drooping leaves up to 18 times as long as broad and reaching 25cm when mature: they are dark green and hairless above and silvery beneath with turned-over margins. The catkins, which appear before the leaves in March or early April, are stalkless, c.3cm long, and clustered near the tips of twigs.

Osier is native on river banks and in damp alluvial soils in valleys, avoiding strongly acid soils: also widely planted for basket making. An attractive garden shrub because of its

early catkins, it can be maintained at an acceptable size by annual 'coppicing' which produces long, straight, grey-hairy stems. Grows best in open situations and is tolerant of smoky atmospheres. Propagated, like other willows, by taking hardwood cuttings in autumn.

Particularly valuable for early flying bees and wasps because its catkins open before most other sources of nectar and pollen are available. The leaves, like those of other willows, are fed on by a large number of caterpillars which provide protein for small birds.

Sambucus nigra elder

One of our most flower-laden, summer shrubs up to 10m tall, elder is recognised before flowering by its thick, furrowed bark and opposite leaves each divided into 5–7 toothed, elliptic leaflets, 3–9 cm long. The small, creamy-white flowers have five joined petals clustered into flat-topped 'plates' and appear in June and July. The flowers are fragrant and develop into round black elder 'berries'.

Widespread in woods, scrub, hedgerows and waste places throughout Scotland, though only an introduction in the northern isles and absent above c.450m in the mountains. Most frequent on lime-rich soils and those high in nitrogen e.g. around old farm buildings.

A shrub no garden should be without – for the beauty and fragrance of its summer flowers and colour of the berries in autumn. Both are consumable – elder-flower cordial makes a cooling drink which carries the scents of summer through the winter, whilst elderberry wine brings inner warmth on cold

days. Easily propagated from hardwood cuttings taken in autumn which can be planted out the following year.

The flowers produce nectar which attracts pollinating flies and beetles, whilst the fruit is relished by blackbirds, greenfinches and summer visitors like blackcaps. Swallowtail moths and common butterflies enjoy the fermenting juice.

Sorbus aucuparia
rowan or mountain ash

A small tree up to 15m with smooth bark, and leaves made up of 9–19 toothed leaflets, 3–6cm long. The creamy-white flowers, which appear after the leaves in May and June, have five separate petals and are borne in large, flat clusters. They produce berries which are yellow at first, then orange, finally ripening to red in September.

Rowan is common on light, free-draining soils in scrub and woodland in the lowlands but is also widespread on rocks and in acid peat in the mountains where it ascends to over 1000m.

A splendid tree for a garden of any size with attractive flowers and berries, and foliage which gives superb autumn colour – gold and red – often persisting until November. It can be maintained at a suitable size by coppicing. Best propagated from seed by gathering berries just before they ripen, storing them in polythene bags until rotten. They should then be washed and the seeds sown in moist sand. Thin and transplant to 1m apart, planting in the final position two years later.

The flowers have a heavy scent which attracts many flies, bees and beetles to feed on the abundant nectar and pollen they produce. The berries provide winter food for larger birds, especially members of the thrush family.

Taxus baccata yew

An evergreen conifer easily recognised by its flat, needle-like leaves, dark-green above and bluish-green beneath. When untrained it can become a medium sized tree up to 20m, but is often maintained as a dense bush by human or wind cutting. One of the few conifers producing leafy branches from an old trunk. Male and female flowers are often borne on separate trees but can occur on the

same one. They open in February or March when the males are conspicuous because of their yellow pollen. The obscure females develop solitary seeds surrounded by a fleshy red 'aril'. The seeds are poisonous but the flesh is not. The leaves are poisonous to

livestock, especially when cut and dried.

Yew is rare as a native in Scotland but place names suggest it was once more widespread in the SW Highlands. It is widely introduced however and thrives well on well-drained soils so long as they are moist in winter.

Particularly valuable as a hedging plant, it is generally frost-resistant though young growth may be killed by late frosts. To ensure male and female progeny it is best raised from cuttings taken in autumn and grown in a cold frame for potting on and later planting out.

The pollen is a valuable food for early-flying honey-bees whilst the fleshy arils are a feast for larger birds, especially mistle thrushes in winter. The dense canopy provides nest sites, and cover for birds throughout the year.

Ulex europaeus gorse

A densely prickly shrub up to 2.5m. Though young plants have clover-like leaves those on the upright branches are reduced to short, sharp, deeply-furrowed spines. Pea-like, deep-yellow flowers appear in March and flowering continues until June or later. Black pods 15mm long develop which open explosively in July.

Gorse grows throughout Scotland, except the far north, on dry, usually acid soils on cliffs, dunes and heaths ascending to c.500m.

A wonderful, golden garden shrub which can be enjoyed as a single specimen or be used as a hedging plant where its spines form a very effective barrier against man and animals. As it is very tolerant of wind and drought but susceptible to frost damage, it is particularly suitable for gardens in the west or near the coast. The bark provides a yellow dye for tartan cloth. Easily raised from seed sown soon after ripening, preferably two or three in a pot leaving the strongest to be planted out the following autumn.

The dense growth is excellent cover for small birds and the prickles protect nest sites. The flowers have a rich coconut smell which attracts honey-bees and bumble-bees to feed

on the pollen. The thorns are food for the caterpillars of the green hairstreak butterfly.

Ulex gallii western gorse

An autumn flowering shrub similar to gorse, but often prostrate with only faintly furrowed spines and smaller flowers than gorse, up to

13mm rather than 20mm. The pods too are smaller, up to 10mm rather than 15mm, and burst in the spring.

Western gorse is rare as a native in Scotland confined to acid soils in Galloway and a few other lowland localities in the Southern Uplands, and to shores on the south side of the Moray Firth. In its coastal localities it is a prominent and eye-catching constituent of the dwarf shrub heath community dominated by heather and bell heather.

A valuable garden shrub giving extended, glorious, golden autumn colour and particularly suitable for exposed coastal localities in the west as, though frost sensitive, it is extremely tolerant of wind. Like gorse it is easily raised from seed, collected after the pods ripen in April and May, so long as they are sown two to three to a pot leaving the best to be planted out the following spring.

Important as a source of pollen for honey-bees and bumble-bees in autumn, and for providing cover for ground-nesting and - feeding birds.

Viburnum opulus guelder-rose

A handsome, deciduous shrub up to 4m which is recognised throughout the growing season by its large, broad, irregularly-lobed leaves arranged in opposite pairs, in early summer by its large plates of flowers each with five joined petals, large, white and sterile on the outside, creamy-white and fertile in the centre, and in autumn by its round, red juicy berries.

Guelder-rose flourishes in moist, moderately acid or alkaline soils at the margins of woods or in scrub in many parts of lowland Scotland but is absent from the outer isles and the far north.

An extremely attractive shrub for any garden with beautiful flowers, colourful berries, and leaves which often turn red or yellow in autumn. It flowers best in open sun or only light shade. Readily raised from seed collected in the autumn, stratified during the winter and sown in early March: can also be raised from cuttings taken in late summer and transferred to pots the following spring. An important wildlife habitat: the nectar in the flowers is very attractive to hover-flies whilst the berries, though slightly poisonous to man, are popular with birds.

WILD FLOWERS

Achillea millefolium yarrow

A common and attractive perennial recognised by its leaves, long and narrow in outline but divided into hundreds of feathery segments. From July onwards it produces shoots up to 50cm tall topped by flat clusters of white, pink and, occasionally, purple flower-heads. Each 'flower' is 4–6mm across with c.5 ray florets and many creamy-white tubular florets.

Yarrow grows wild in rough grassland on well-drained, moderately acid to calcareous soils throughout Scotland and up to 1200m in the Highlands. It is very drought resistant.

The attractive leaves and long flowering season make this an excellent species for a 'meadow' as well as for the lawn which it will help keep green in a dry summer: also recommended for the herbaceous border where the pink and purple varieties are particularly suitable. One of our most important medicinal plants both as an infusion and for bathing wounds. Easily raised from seed or by dividing plants in spring or autumn. Widely available from nurseries.

The caterpillars of several species of tortricoid moths feed on the roots, stems and leaves as far north as Shetland, whilst the flowers are visited by numerous hover-flies and bees.

Achillea ptarmica sneezewort

A perennial herb with creeping roots which grows to 60cm. It is closely related to yarrow with similar flower-heads but larger, up to 18mm across with eight to 15 showy ray florets which appear in July and August, but is readily distinguished from yarrow by the leaves which are long, narrow and undivided with a fine, small-toothed, saw-like edge.

Sneezewort grows in wet meadows, marshes and on streamsides, on slightly acid soils throughout Scotland ascending to 650m in the Highlands.

An attractive garden herb especially suitable for damp corners and pond margins. A double form known as Batchelor's Buttons is available from nurseries and is particularly showy. Easily raised from seed or propagated by splitting the root-stock and planting out in the required position in spring or autumn.

The flowers produce nectar which is attractive to many species of beetle, butterflies and moths though the double form has little nectar to offer. Many species of moth caterpillars feed on the roots, stems and leaves.

Ajuga reptans bugle

A creeping, almost hairless perennial up to 30cm, similar to selfheal (*Prunella vulgaris*) with dark-purple, rounded leaves in opposite pairs and short dense spikes of blue flowers, but bugle has no upper lip whereas selfheal has a hood above.

Bugle grows in alder and other damp woods and also in meadows. It tolerates deep shade to full sun and can be found throughout Scotland except for some parts of the far north and Shetland, reaching 650m in the Highlands.

A most attractive garden plant for the front of the border or a shady shrubbery, so long as its ability to spread is controlled. It flowers in spring and summer and the purple leaves provide colour the year round. An infusion from the leaves mixed with peppermint makes a powerful tonic. Easily propagated by division in spring or autumn or from seed sown outdoors in April. Widely available from nurseries.

The large tubular flowers produce nectar which is fed on by hover-flies, bees and many species of butterflies. From July onwards the upper leaves and flowers are sometimes attacked by a gall-mite which causes distortion and the production of a mass of white hairs by the plant.

Alchemilla alpina alpine lady's-mantle

A procumbent perennial, easily distinguished by its attractive leaves, each with five to seven narrow leaflets, green above and silvery-hairy beneath. The yellow-green flowers are arranged in heads, each flower with four sepals but no petals. The seed is set without fertilisation so that all plants raised from seed are almost identical to the parent plant.

Common in dwarf shrub heath on exposed

base-rich rocks where snow lies late, throughout the Highlands, ascending to 1200m on Ben Lawers in Perthshire and on Ben Nevis in Inverness-shire and extending to the outer isles. It often grows in close association with *Sibbaldia procumbens*, another member of the rose family.

A useful plant for the exposed rock garden with attractive long-lived leaves and a neat, non-vigorous habit. Easily propagated by dividing the root-stock and planting out

where required, or from seed collected in polythene bags placed over flower heads in autumn and sown in spring. Widely available from nurseries.

Though seeds are produced without fertilisation, pollen is necessary to stimulate their formation, and the pollen produced is eaten by stone-flies. The leaves are eaten by the caterpillars of a common mountain tortricoid moth, the aptly named *Acleris caledoniana*.

Allium ursinum ramsons

Although by its smell an 'onion', it differs from other species because it has broad, ovate, basal leaves similar to lily-of-the-valley. The white, star-like flowers have six petals and stamens and are arranged in flat-topped clusters on long leafless stems, up to 45cm, which appear in late spring.

Ramsons often grows in thousands on the floor of damp birch and oak woods and tolerates both acid and alkaline soils. It may be found throughout lowland Scotland, especially in the south and west but is absent from the northern isles.

An attractive plant for the shrubbery or woodland corner where it could be mixed with bluebells by the patriotic gardener. The leaves can be used like chives, finely chopped in salads or for flavouring soups. Easily

propagated, like other onions, by splitting the bulbs, or by sowing the round black seeds in damp leaf mould in the area where they are to be established. Available from one or two nurseries.

The nectar attracts flies, honey-bees and two species of fritillary butterfly, the pearl-bordered and the small pearl-bordered. The leaves may be food for syrphid flies.

Anemone nemorosa wood anemone

Flowering stems with three, small, divided leaves appear from March to May carrying solitary white or pink-tinged flowers with sepals varying in number from five to 12 (mainly six or seven). One or two larger leaves

grow from the ground after flowering and persist until mid-summer when the rest of the plant has died down.

Wood anemone often grows in carpets in hedge bottoms or on the floor of deciduous woods, mainly birch and oak, but also occurs in the open in dwarf shrub heathland above the tree-line ascending to 1,200m on Ben

Lawers in Perthshire. It is found throughout Scotland except the far north-east and the northern isles.

A splendid plant for a sunlit shrubbery brightening up a corner before the bushes come into leaf. Once established it spreads by slender, brown rhizomes which rest underground during autumn and winter. Propagated by division in March or October or by root cuttings taken in spring. Widely available from nurseries.

The flowers droop in damp weather, and at night, protecting the abundant pollen they produce, which is invaluable for early flying honey-bees, bumble-bees, beetles and several families of flies.

Antennaria dioica mountain everlasting

A small perennial up to 20cm tall recognised by its compact rosettes of leaves, usually several together, white woolly beneath and broadest near the top, and the flowering

shoots carrying much narrower leaves. The heads of tubular flowers, which open in mid-summer, are clustered at the top – the white males and rose-pink females on separate plants.

Mountain everlasting grows on heaths, dunes, dry pastures and rocky mountain slopes throughout Scotland, but is much more common in the Highlands and Islands than in the lowlands, ascending to 850m on Ben Hope in Sutherland.

A most attractive species for the rock garden or on dry walls with year-round silvery rosettes which are persistent without being aggressive. Easily propagated by separating the rosettes, which root at the base, and planting them out in spring. It is available from many nurseries as is an unusual form, var. *hyperborea* with broader leaves and woolly-white hairs on both surfaces, which is found wild in the Inner and Outer Hebrides.

An infusion of the heads, collected in July and then dried, is an antidote to gall bladder complaints and acts as a febrifuge.

Anthyllis vulneraria **kidney vetch**

An erect or sprawling, hairy perennial up to 60cm with leaves of three to nine leaflets, the largest at the top. The pea-like flowers are arranged in clusters – two together at the top of a stalk: they are very variable in colour and white, cream, yellow and crimson

varieties are known. After flowering the calyx enlarges to form a persistent woolly head.

Scattered throughout Scotland in dry places on shallow, usually lime-rich soils and particularly abundant round the coast where it forms carpets in sand dunes and on cliff tops.

A useful herb with a wide range of colours to choose from for the rock garden or a sunny free-draining border. As the name implies, a 'vulnerary' formerly used for soothing slow-healing wounds, cuts and bruises when applied as a compress to the affected area. Easily propagated by division in the autumn or from seed down in situ in spring. Widely available from nurseries.

The flowers are a rich source of nectar but it is only accessible to larger insects like bumble-bees, strong enough to force them open. The caterpillars of the small blue butterfly feed on the leaves and may be seen along north-east coasts.

Armeria maritima **thrift**

An unmistakable perennial with numerous long, narrow, grass-like but fleshy leaves arising from a woody rootstock. Often making a dense cushion from which leafless, hairy, grooved stalks arise up to 25cm, ending in dense, hemispherical heads of 5-petalled pink (or occasionally white) flowers surrounded by a ring of chaff-like bracts.

Thrift is found on cliffs, rocks and in salt marshes all round the coast of Scotland, but also up to 1280m on mountains inland, almost to the top of Ben Nevis.

A very reliable performer in the well-drained herbaceous border or rock-garden with a long flowering season and heads which can be dried and used in flower arranging. Propagated by dividing the root-stock in autumn or spring or from seed sown in spring in a sandy soil. Widely available from nurseries.

With flowers producing both nectar and pollen, thrift is good for bumble-bees and is also attractive to hover-flies and gall-midges. The leaves are fed on by the caterpillars of several species of tortricoid moth.

Caltha palustris marsh-marigold

A creeping perennial up to 50cm with leaves which are kidney-shaped, dark-green with a toothed margin, and large 'buttercup' flowers 4–5cm across with five to eight yellow petal-like sepals which appear from March to July. Each flower produces up to ten pods (follicles) c.15mm long which split open to release the seeds before they are dry.

Marsh-marigold is widespread in marshes, on stream banks and in wet woods throughout Scotland ascending to over 1100m on Lochnagar.

An excellent species for a garden pond, preferably in partial shade, so that the soil never dries out. The unopened golden flower buds were once gathered and pickled and eaten as a substitute for capers and could be tried again. Known as water gowan or gowland in Scotland – gowan was a medieval word for a yellow flower. Readily propagated by division and planting out in showery weather in autumn or by sowing seed in spring. Widely available from nurseries.

Visited by many species of insect including early bumble-bees and stoneflies both for its nectar and its pollen. Avoid the 'flora pleno' form in which nectaries have become 'petals'.

Campanula glomerata clustered bellflower

A handsome perennial up to 20cm, recognised by its long-stalked, toothed, basal leaves and short, hairy, erect, crimson stems with stalkless leaves. Each stem terminates in a cluster of erect, clustered bell-shaped flowers each up to 2.5cm across. The flowers are usually blue-purple but occasionally white and appear in July and August.

Clustered bellflower is a rare species in Scotland confined to base-rich grassland on sea-cliffs and sand dunes on the east coast from East Lothian north to Kincardineshire. A superb plant for free-draining, sunny, herbaceous borders which is easy to grow in the drier parts of the country: the shorter var. *acaulis* may be preferred. Readily propagated by division in the autumn or from seed sown on fine compost and not covered by soil. Widely available from nurseries.

Stamens open before the flowers and deposit pollen on the hairy outside of the stigmas. Visiting bees seeking nectar are dusted by the pollen which they carry to the next flower but, if no insect arrives, the stigmas curl back onto their own pollen and self-fertilisation occurs.

Campanula latifolia giant bellflower

A tall, robust perennial up to 1m with angled stems and oval, toothed leaves, broadest at the base. The stems are terminated by leafy spikes of large blue-purple flowers, often over 4cm long, from July onwards. These develop into egg-shaped nodding capsules which

shed their seed through pores at the base.

Giant bellflower flourishes in damp woodland and on river banks through much of lowland Scotland up to 350m, but is absent from the north and north-west and from all the outer isles.

With flowers as big as a Canterbury-bell, this is a handsome species for the back of a shady border or naturalised in woodland where both blue and white forms show to advantage against a dark background. The shoots can be peeled, cooked and eaten like spinach. Easily propagated by division in the autumn or raised from seed as for clustered bellflower. Both blue and white forms are widely available from nurseries.

Anthers produce pollen before the stigmas are mature and visiting bees, seeking nectar, act as pollinators.

Campanula rotundifolia bluebell or harebell

This is the commonest of all the bellflowers. Although it has only narrow leaves on its upright stems, the Latin name *rotundifolia* is justified by the small, round leaves at the base of the stem though these are often difficult to

see. The 30cm tall stems bear one or two blue, bell-like flowers 15mm long on slender stalks: they are erect in bud but nodding when open.

It is found throughout Scotland in short grassland on both acid and alkaline soils from sea-level to over 1150m in the Breadalbane mountains of Perthshire. Less common in the far north and absent from Orkney.

A charming little plant for the rock garden on any soil or for naturalising in a wild meadow so long as the grass is kept short. Best propagated by division in autumn or by sowing seed as for clustered bellflower. Available from a number of nurseries.

Known in Gaelic as brog na cubhaig, the cuckoo's shoe, but not normally visited by creatures larger than bumble-bees attracted by the nectar. The leaves are fed on by the caterpillars of two species of rustic moth.

Cardamine pratensis cuckooflower

Creeping perennial herb up to 60cm with a basal rosette of hairless leaves divided into segments like watercress with the terminal lobe largest. It is recognised in early spring from a distance as large patches of lilac. The 4-petalled flowers, up to 18mm across, have petals three times as long as the sepals. These develop into long, narrow cress-like pods up to 5cm long.

Cuckooflower grows in damp meadows, marshes, reed-beds, stream banks and loch-sides throughout Scotland to 1000m on Ben Lawers in Perthshire.

An attractive species for the shady bog garden, pond or stream margin giving an early splash of colour. A white form also occurs: large patches of this were said to resemble linen bleaching in the sun and hence another name, lady's-smock. The leaves not only look like watercress, but can be eaten in salads in its place. Propagate by dividing the rootstock in autumn or sowing seed in April. Available from many nurseries but the sterile, double form should be avoided.

The nectar-rich flowers attract bee-flies and hover-flies which have proboscis long enough to reach the bottom of the large tubular flowers. Often covered in foam produced by frog-hopper nymphs called 'cuckoo-spit' which may be the origin of the name cuckooflower. The leaves are food for the caterpillars of orange-tip butterflies.

Centaurea nigra common knapweed

A hairy, perennial herb up to 60cm with lance-shaped, sometimes lobed, leaves. It is recognised by its reddish-purple, normally tubular, flowers (florets) arranged in hard, compact heads surrounded by blackish-brown bracts each with a fringe of black hairs. More attractive forms occur in which the outer 'ray' florets are large and more showy though sterile. Flowers first appear in June and continue through the summer.

Knapweed is common in rough grassland, on

road verges and in hedgerows on a wide range of soils throughout most of Scotland but is absent from Shetland and above 550m in the Highlands.

The very attractive 'rayed' form is excellent for the middle of the herbaceous border but also naturalises well in a wild meadow corner. Also known as 'hardheads' because of the way the flowers are protected, it is easily raised by sowing seed gathered from these heads and sown in March or April. It may also be propagated by division in the spring. Available from a few nurseries.

Very important for wildlife because the flowers produce nectar which attracts hover-flies, bees and many species of butterfly including tortoiseshells and painted ladies and the ripe seeds provide winter food for finches. The stems may produce swellings as a reaction to attacks by gall wasps and the leaves are enjoyed by the caterpillars of several species of tortricoid moth.

Cirsium vulgare spear thistle

Although treated as a weed, this thistle is handsome and the one usually used to depict the Scottish Thistle on coins, medals and other memorabilia – and much more appropriate as the so-called Scottish Thistle

does not grow wild in Scotland and is not even native in England!

A biennial with a large basal rosette of spiny, ground-hugging leaves from which a single spiny-winged stem rises up to 1.5m. This carries leaves with thorn-like tips and large heads made up of many narrow bracts enclosing pale, reddish-purple florets.

Spear thistle is widespread throughout Scotland in scrub, grassland and waste places on moderately acid to neutral soils from sea-shore to over 700m in the Highlands.

This is a species to promote in the wild garden where it should be tolerated, not only for patriotic reasons, but as an important wildlife habitat and, it is claimed, because its young flower shoots can be eaten as a vegetable.

The florets produce nectar and pollen which attract a large number of honey-bees and bumble-bees, ladybirds, flies and butterflies such as painted ladies which will appear in August and September and whose caterpillars also feed on the leaves along with those of several tortricoid moths. In addition, the seed-heads in autumn may bring you a charm of goldfinches.

Convallaria majalis lily-of-the-valley

A creeping perennial with extensive underground rhizomes and therefore often appears as large patches of glossy, hairless,

oval leaves. Out of these, in spring, grow leafless stalks which carry the familiar, fragrant, hanging, bell-like, white flowers which develop into red berries.

A rare and local Scottish plant, almost literally the lily-of-the-valley, growing on river banks and in lowland woods from Ayrshire north to East Inverness. The Latin name, *Convallaria*, also reflects its association with valleys.

A familiar and much-loved garden plant of great value for a damp, shady border or for naturalising in grass beneath trees, which provides sweet-scented posies in May. It is also the source of a drug used in homoeopathy for treating various heart conditions. Propagated by division and planted out in October and November in good quality soil with plenty of well-rotted compost. Widely available from nurseries.

The flowers produce no nectar but the scent attracts many insects including honey-bees which take the pollen. If pollination fails the flowers are selfed. Beware, the berries are poisonous.

Cruciata laevipes crosswort

A scrambling, hairy perennial instantly recognised by the yellowish-green colour of the whole plant and by the pointed petals and elliptical leaves arranged in fours, which may have given the plant its name. The flowers are arranged in clusters in the angle of the leaves and first appear in May. They are unusual as, in each cluster, the outer flowers are male and only the central ones are hermaphrodite and capable of producing the black fruits on turned-down stalks which develop in later summer.

Crosswort is extremely abundant in open woods, scrub and hedgerows, usually on heavy, base-rich soils, in the south and east of Scotland as far north as Angus, with a few scattered localities round the Moray Firth.

This attractive species, which emits a strong scent of honey, will brighten a shady hedge bottom or grace the margin of a pond. Easily propagated by division in the autumn. Available from very few nurseries.

The scent attracts many pollinating bees and flies whilst the leaves are food for the caterpillars of several species of hawk, dart and rustic moths.

Dianthus deltoides maiden pink

A loosley-tufted, creeping perennial with shoots bearing short, narrow, opposite leaves and terminating, usually, in single flowers with five, toothed and white-spotted, pink petals. As with other pinks, the petals are enclosed in a leathery, tubular calyx.

A rare and declining species, of sand dunes and grassy cliffs. Mainly coastal, it is confined to the east of Scotland north to Kincardineshire where it reaches its northern limit in Britain.

A charming small pink, with its rich-coloured, though scentless, flowers suitable for a sunny position in the rock garden on lime-rich soil. Propagated from cuttings taken immediately after flowering, dusted with growth hormone and inserted in pure sand round the rim of a pot and protected until roots form. When planted out it needs netting against rabbits if you have them as they are very partial to pinks. Available from several nurseries.

Many butterflies with long proboscis are attracted to the nectar hidden at the base of the stamens, but the tough calyx prevents theft 'through the back door' by biting insects. The low-growing tussocks often shelter wolf spiders.

Digitalis purpurea foxglove

One of our most familiar wild flowers recognised before it flowers by the basal rosette of softly hairy, elliptical leaves from which rises a leafy stalk. The latter bears a long inflorescence of large, nodding, tubular pink or purple flowers, often with spots in the throat which open at the bottom in May and produce new flowers higher and higher until September.

Foxglove grows wild on heaths and rocks and in open woodland on acid soils throughout Scotland, except Shetland, rising to 650m in Atholl.

A magnificent garden plant invaluable for the back of the herbaceous border or for naturalising in a wooded corner but, beware, all parts are poisonous, though the drug digitalis, prepared from the dried leaves, is valued in the treatment of certain heart conditions. As a biennial it is best propagated by sowing some of the copious seed in April or May, transferring seedlings to a shady, holding bed in July and planting in their final position in autumn. A white-flowered form may be preferred and is available, along with the purple, in many nurseries.

The nectar attracts bumble-bees which pollinate the flowers as they work their way up the finger of the 'fox glove' whilst the leaves are food for caterpillars of lesser yellow underwing and Ashworth's rustic moth.

Dryas octopetala mountain avens

A dwarf prostrate shrub with many small, stalked, oblong, oak-like leaves with rounded

teeth at the margin, dark-green above but white-hairy beneath. Large, 8-petalled white flowers, up to 4cm across, appear in June developing, in fruit, to a compact head of achenes with long, persistent, hooked styles.

Mountain avens grows on limestone or other basic soils in dwarf shrub heath in the Inner Hebrides and in the Highlands up to 975m but also occurs at sea level on the north coast west of Thurso.

An invaluable plant for the limestone rock garden in a peaty compost forming large, ground-hugging patches attractive in leaf, flower or fruit. Herbal tea made from dried leaves is a stomach tonic but if you feel you want to spit it out, try it as a gargle too! Probably most easily propagated by division of the self-rooting branchlets but cuttings may also be taken and rooted in sandy soil in August. Plants can be raised from seed sown in a cold frame in April or May. Widely available from nurseries.

Pollinated by small insects attracted to the nectar at the base of the many stamens. The leaves may be mined by the larva of a small moth, *Stigmella dryadella*. This plant with its oak-like leaves (and the moth) were named after Dryad, the nymph of the oak tree.

Echium vulgare viper's-bugloss

An erect, hairy biennial with a basal rosette of narrow leaves with prominent midribs, from which arises, in summer, a spike of vivid-blue, funnel-shaped flowers with four to five stamens that are longer than the petals. Each flower develops four triangular nutlets around the base of the style.

Viper's-bugloss is local below 350m in south and east Scotland north to the shores of the Moray Firth. It grows in dry soils on sea cliffs and river banks, and in sand dunes and waste places.

A brilliant garden plant for a sunny position in the middle of the herbaceous border. The young leaves and shoots can be collected and eaten like spinach though, in the Tyrol,

people are warned not to as it stimulates sexual desire. Easily propagated by sowing seed in well drained soil in late spring and planting out in the autumn for flowering the following summer. Available from several nurseries.

Important for wildlife because the amazing colour and the scent of the flowers, which are full of nectar, attract large numbers of bees, butterflies and moths.

Empetrum nigrum crowberry

A low, trailing evergreen shrub, up to 20cm, with tiny, crowded, bright green, shiny, heath-like, leaves with turned back margins which hide the underside. Pinkish-purple flowers appear in clusters near the end of the stems in May and June. In most places there are separate male and female plants: male flowers have bright red stamens whilst the females develop black, inedible berries. On

the higher mountains, however, plants have both male and female flowers.

Crowberry is abundant in bogs and on heaths and mountain tops throughout Scotland ascending to 1300m and often dominating large areas.

A useful evergreen shrub for an acid, shaded rock garden or boggy area. Best propagated by inserting cuttings in a sandy peat substitute during the summer in a cool, shaded frame and planting out in the spring. Available from a few nurseries.

Though man finds the 'crow black' berries unpalatable when they ripen in late summer, they are a major food source for ptarmigan, grouse and other moorland birds. The leaves are enjoyed by the caterpillars of several moths including northern dart, broad-bordered white underwing and black mountain.

Filipendula ulmaria meadowsweet

An erect, sweet-smelling herb with strongly-veined basal leaves divided into two to five pairs of toothed, ovate segments and with similar, though less divided, stem leaves. The stems terminate in a feathery mass of small, creamy-white, 5-petalled flowers which develop into clusters of fruits curiously, spirally twisted together.

Meadowsweet lives up to its name growing in wet meadows throughout Scotland, as well as in ditches and along river banks, and ascending to over 900m in the Breadalbane Mountains of Perthshire.

A most attractive species for a damp, sunlit corner of the wild garden or round the margin of a pond. Not only are the flowers scented but the leaves, when crushed, emit an aroma of oil of wintergreen and were strewn on the floors of medieval houses to hide less pleasant odours. 'Meadowsweet' may be derived from 'Mede Sweet' because the flowers were formerly used to flavour mead and could be used today in home-made wines. Propagated by division in spring or by sowing seeds in a cold frame as soon as they have ripened in autumn. Widely available from nurseries.

The numerous stamens produce abundant pollen which attracts many insects including crane-flies, midges and short-tongued flies. The leaves are food for the caterpillars of glaucous shears, hebrew character and powdered quaker moths.

Fragaria vesca wild strawberry

Closely related to the garden strawberry but only growing to about 30cm and with smaller, sweeter fruits. The leaves are stalked and

divided into three elliptical toothed segments. The white, 5-petalled flowers appear in April and May and the berries are ripe in mid-summer.

Wild strawberries may be found in scrub, open woods and hedges throughout Scotland up to 600m, but they are local in the north and absent from Shetland.

A useful, self-sustaining plant for a hedge-bottom or a wooded bank, with delectable fruit sweet enough to pick and eat straightaway. The dried leaves make an excellent tea substitute. Although the name 'strawberry' may refer to the practise of growing them in straw to prevent rotting, it is just as likely to be derived from 'strew berry' from its habit of spreading by long runners. Easily propagated by detaching these long runners, which root at the nodes, and planting them out in autumn. Available from many nurseries.

A valuable food for wildlife – if we do not eat the berries other mammals, birds and the strawberry snail will. The flower buds are relished by weevils whilst pollen-seeking beetles help fertilisation. The leaves may be mined by the larvae of small moths.

Galium odoratum woodruff

A perennial herb, with long creeping underground stems, forming large patches from which arise simple stems up to c.45cm, with whorls of six to eight narrow, elliptical leaves with forwardly pointed marginal prickles. The stems are topped by a loose cluster of tiny white flowers, each with four joined petals, which appear in late spring and early summer and develop into round, rough fruits with hooked, black-tipped bristles.

Woodruff occurs in oak and other damp woods on moderately acid to base-rich soils throughout most of Scotland ascending to 650m in Atholl, but it is local in the north and absent, as a native, from the outer isles.

As a garden plant it must be kept away from the rock garden because of its penetrating underground stems, but is ideal for the shady woodland corner or hedge bottom, with flowers emitting a most fragrant scent like new-mown hay. Very easily propagated by division in autumn. Widely available from nurseries.

The scent attracts many pollinating flies, bees and sawflies which feed on the easily accessible nectar whilst the leaves are food for caterpillars of various species of hawk and dart moths.

Geranium pratense
meadow crane's-bill

This handsome perennial, up to 70cm, is easily recognised by the much-dissected leaves, round in outline (characteristic of all crane's-bills) and the pairs of large 5-petalled violet-blue, crimson-veined flowers as much as 4cm across. These develop the familiar long-beaked fruits, the crane's-bill, containing five wrinkled seeds shed by an

extraordinary explosive mechanism – five strips of the fruit wall suddenly curl up and fling out the seeds.

Meadow crane's-bill is widespread in meadows and on roadsides in moderately acid to basic soils. It is found throughout southern and eastern Scotland north to the southern shores of the Moray Firth and reaches 500m near Ballater, but is absent from the north and west.

This is a magnificent plant for the middle of the herbaceous border or for naturalising in a grassy verge, with brilliant flowers throughout the summer, often flowering a second time after cutting back. Easily propagated by division in spring or autumn or by raising from seed sown in a cold frame or in the open in early spring. Widely available from nurseries including a white form.

The concealed nectar attracts bumble-bees, honey-bees and solitary wasps which are the main pollinators, as they brush their bodies over the anthers of the upright stamens.

Geranium sanguineum
bloody crane's-bill

A low-growing perennial with narrowly-lobed leaves dissected to the leaf-stalk. Solitary flowers (not pairs as in other crane's-bills) are produced on long stalks, up to 3cm across with, usually, bright purplish-crimson (bloody) petals, though pink and white

forms occasionally occur. In this and other crane's-bills the ten stamens ripen first and all their pollen is shed before the stigma opens to expose five pollen-receptive lobes.

Bloody crane's-bill is mainly a coastal plant in Scotland where it grows in base-rich cliff grassland and on sand dunes where a more prostrate variety is recognised.

A well-loved garden plant giving excellent colour and cover in the limestone rock garden, where the prostrate form is particularly suitable, or in a sunny, well-drained, herbaceous border. Propagated by division or by sowing seed as for meadow crane's-bill. Widely available from nurseries including the prostrate form (var. *prostrata*), the pink (var. *lancastriense*) and the white ('Album').

Like other crane's-bills, the veins on the petals act as honey guides directing visiting bumble- and honey-bees to the source of nectar. These and saw-flies are the main pollinators.

Geranium sylvaticum
wood crane's-bill

A bushy perennial, up to 80cm tall, similar to meadow crane's-bill but differing in having less dissected leaves, smaller, more reddish-violet flowers, up to 3cm across, and upright, not drooping, young fruits (crane's-bills).

Wood crane's-bill is widespread in tall, herb-rich vegetation often on steep, base-rich

rocks out of the reach of grazing animals, mainly south of the Great Glen above 300m and reaching 900m on the Breadalbane Mountains of Perthshire.

A charming plant for a damp, shady border where the white var. *album* may show to advantage against a dark background. Easily propagated by division or by sowing seed as for other perennial crane's-bills. Widely available from nurseries in a variety of shades.

As long ago as 1787 the German botanist Sprengel observed that there are hairs on the petals which prevent the nectar from being diluted by rain so that, after the storm has passed, the all important pollinating bees are still attracted to the flowers.

Geum rivale water avens

A tufted perennial, up to 60cm, with mainly basal leaves divided into three to six pairs of unequal, toothed segments, the terminal largest, and a few simple leaves on the stem. In summer the stems produce nodding flowers on long stalks which have five orange petals largely hidden by a purple calyx. These develop into compact heads of achenes hooked at the tip.

Water avens grows throughout Scotland, mainly on base-rich soils, in marshes, wet woods and on damp rock ledges particularly

out of the reach of grazing animals, rising to over 900m in Rannoch.

A charming and not too aggressive species for pond margins or damp wooded corners. *Geum* comes from a Greek word meaning 'I taste' and Culpeper says the root has 'a delicate flavour and taste' that 'comforteth the heart'. An infusion of the dried roots is a herbal remedy for various disorders of stomach and liver. Easily propagated by division in spring or autumn or from seed sown out of doors in April and May. Widely available from nurseries.

Nectaries hidden by the large number of stamens attract honey-bees and bumble-bees which are the main pollinators. The leaves are eaten by the caterpillars of a number of small moths.

Glechoma hederacea ground-ivy

A creeping perennial herb, not related to ivy, which has square stems and heart-shaped leaves in opposite pairs. The short ascending stems which reach 30cm produce, from May

onwards, 2-lipped, bright-blue flowers with purple-spotted lower lips, arranged in one-sided clusters of two to four flowers up to 20mm long, but female plants with much smaller, earlier flowers also occur.

Ground-ivy is found in woods, hedgebanks, grassland and waste places throughout much of lowland Scotland, but is absent from most of the north and west and does not occur as a native in the outer isles.

A showy plant for naturalising in an orchard or other sunlit, wooded corner forming patches of colour in spring and early summer. Once used in brewing to clear bitter beer in place of hops, it makes an excellent herbal tea if drunk with plenty of sugar to offset the bitter flavour. Easily propagated by division in spring or by raising from seed. Available from several nurseries including a variegated form.

Mainly pollinated by bumble-bees, but also visited by bee-flies which take the hidden nectar but are too small to pollinate the wide-throated flowers. The leaves may be attacked by a gall-midge; they respond by making light-coloured cylinders known as 'Lighthouse galls'. Other pea-sized lumps are caused by a gall wasp.

Helianthemum nummularium
common rock-rose

A familiar, prostrate dwarf shrub with oval leaves, dark-green above but white-hairy beneath. The large, yellow, 5-petalled flowers have many stamens and, in common with other members of the *Cistus* family, the petals last for only a day and the ground around them is littered with their confetti-like remains.

Rock-rose is common in south and east Scotland north to the Moray Firth, on sea cliffs, and inland on base-rich rocks, in grassland and grass heath, ascending to 640m in Atholl.

No rock garden would be complete without this plant which produces such a blaze of colour in summer but remains green and compact for the rest of the year: it can also be used to cover walls or dry banks. Easily propagated from cuttings of young shoots taken in summer, dusted with rooting hormone and inserted in a sandy compost and, when rooted, transferred to small pots and planted out, from the pots, the following spring. Widely available from nurseries in a variety of colour forms.

Valuable for bees which are attracted first by the colour and then by the nectar. The leaves are food for the caterpillars of green hairstreak and Scotch brown argus butterflies and several moths.

Hyacinthoides non-scripta
wild hyacinth or bluebell

Instantly recognised by its long, narrow, basal leaves and the juicy, leafless stalks, drooping at the tip. These appear in spring reaching up to 50cm tall and carrying a spike of blue,

occasionally white, bell-shaped flowers made up of six segments joined at the base and bearing six stamens with cream anthers. Later in summer large capsules form, ripen and shed their black seeds, but the dried stalks often persist well into winter.

Wild hyacinths are found throughout lowland Scotland in oak, birch and ash woods, in hedgebanks and on sea-cliffs on damp, moderately acid to base-rich soils, but they are absent from the northern isles.

This is one of our most treasured wild flowers which is easily naturalised in a wooded corner or old orchard to give sheets of blue delight in spring. It is important to select the native *H. non-scripta* and avoid the introduced, more blousey, *H. hispanica* which has an erect, not drooping, flowering stem, and blue anthers. Easily propagated by division of large clumps of bulbs and replanting c.10cm deep in the autumn. Widely available from nurseries.

Nectar attracts pollinating bumble- and honey-bees, but the latter may 'steal' it by biting a hole near the bottom of the bell rather than entering via the mouth. Also visited by hover-flies and early-flying butterflies. The leaves are enjoyed by the caterpillars of autumnal and six-striped rustic moths.

Hypericum androsaemum tutsan

A semi-evergreen, shrubby plant up to 1m, with stalkless, oval leaves and large yellow, 5-petalled flowers up to 2cm across. Each flower has three large and two small sepals, and many stamens which are arranged in small clusters: they open in July and August. The flowers develop into a berry-like fruit, red at first, but later changing to purple-black and shedding a large amount of seed when dry.

Tutsan is local in Scotland, confined to places near the sea along the west coast and growing in gulleys, on cliffs and woodland margins on damp, moderately acid to base-rich soils.

A valuable, long-flowering species ideal for a border in moderate shade where the soil does not dry out. The dried leaves smell sweetly resinous and have been used as scented bookmarks, whilst the fresh leaves were formerly used to dress cuts and grazes, hence the name Tutsan derived from the French 'toute-saine' (self heal).

Though lacking nectar, the bright colour of the flowers and the abundant pollen produced by the numerous stamens attract many pollen-eating and pollinating beetles and other insects.

Iris pseudacorus yellow iris or flag

Irises differ from lilies in having only three stamens and by often having leaves flattened in one plane – like flags – and by which they

can be easily recognised before the flowers appear in June. These flowers are a striking yellow and clustered in twos and threes at the top of a leafless stem up to 1.5m tall, developing after flowering into large, ribbed, cylindrical capsules over 4cm long.

Yellow irises can be seen throughout Scotland in marshes and on loch margins and in shallow moderately acid to base-rich water from sea-shore to about 300m.

A magnificent plant for pond or stream margin, as fine as any foreign iris, giving colour throughout June and July. The underground rhizome has been used medicinally but it contains poisons and is better left unused. This rhizome, though, can be readily divided into separate plants in spring and will then probably only require lifting and dividing again every three years. Widely available from nurseries.

The whole plant gives shelter to frogs and newts, whilst the leaves are food for the caterpillars of several species of moth. Freshly opened flowers hold their petal-like styles well above the petals and are pollinated by bumble-bees, but a day later the styles lie flat on the petals and only long-tongued hover-flies can reach the nectar.

Jasione montana sheep's-bit

A biennial 'clustered bellflower' with heads of blue flowers, the petals at first tubular, later spreading, surrounded by leafy bracts, and raised up to 30cm on stems bare at the top but with narrow, hairy, wavy-margined, oblong leaves at the base. At the centre of each flower the stamens are joined in a tube through which the female style grows. Each flower produces a capsule which opens by two valves.

Sheep's-bit is common on dry, well-drained, often acid, rocks, grassy sea cliffs and rocky streamsides in south-west Scotland north to the Fort William area, but is otherwise very rare, except in Shetland where it is widespread.

An attractive, small, brightly-coloured addition to a sunny, sandy border which will start flowering in June, but do not crush the leaves as they emit a disagreeable smell. The name 'sheep's-bit' alludes to the way the plant is nibbled by sheep in the rough grassland it grows in. Best raised from seed sown where the plants are to grow. Available from some nurseries.

Pollen is shed into a tube formed by the young petals and pushed out by the elongating style from which it is collected by wasps and other insects attracted by the whole cluster of flowers. The leaves are occasionally food for the caterpillars of tortricoid moths.

Knautia arvensis field scabious

A roughly-hairy perennial up to 1m with deeply-cut stem leaves and long-stalked heads of bluish-lilac, sometimes purple or pink, 4-petalled flowers, the marginal ones often

with larger lobes on the outside. The sepals are reduced to eight bristles which surround a single nut.

Only found frequently on the east side of Scotland north to the Moray Firth but thinly scattered and mainly coastal. Elsewhere it grows generally in dry, ungrazed, usually base-rich grassland on roadsides and railway banks.

A splendid plant for naturalising in a wild meadow area where it competes well with vigorous grasses and gives a colourful display well into autumn. An infusion of the flowers, fresh or dried, may be prescribed for purifying the blood and curing various skin disorders like 'scabies'. Easily propagated by division in March. Available from several nurseries.

An invaluable wildlife plant. The nectar in the flowers attracts a succession of butterflies, bees, beetles and hover-flies whilst the leaves are eaten by the caterpillars of several moths and butterflies.

Lathyrus linifolius bitter-vetch

A perennial herb which produces many tubers underground. It has winged stems and leaves which have two to four pairs of leaflets and end in a short point. The leaflets are usually elliptical but very narrow forms also occur. Spikes of two to six flowers, at first crimson, later becoming green or blue, are arranged on short, hairless stalks and appear in spring and early summer. The hairless pods have 4–10 seeds.

Bitter-vetch is widespread in Scotland in woods, scrub and shady hedgebanks on acid soils and it is mainly lowland though rising to 750m in the Highlands. Absent from the northern isles.

A useful species for naturalising in a shady corner at the bottom of a wooded bank. Formerly cultivated for its tubers which were eaten in the north and west: the flavour is said to resemble chestnuts but is improved if washed down with whisky. Readily propagated by division in the spring or by sowing seed where it is to flower. Not available from nurseries.

Brush-like hairs below the stigma are covered with pollen shed before the flowers open, and this is brushed off by bumble-bees, the main visitors, on their way to collect the nectar, who then transfer it to the next flower.

Lathyrus pratensis yellow vetchling

Easily recognised by having tendrils for clambering up other plants, winged stems and only one or two pairs of leaflets below the tendrils. Yellow vetchling also has a pair of spear-shaped, leaf-like stipules where the leaf-stalk joins the stem. This is the only

common vetchling with yellow flowers, and these are carried in clusters of five to 12 on stout stalks up to 8cm long and produce hairy, flattened, 5–10-seeded pods.

Yellow vetchling occurs in rough grassland and hedgerows on moderately acid to neutral, somewhat damp soils throughout most of Scotland but is absent from the Highlands above about 350m.

A valuable species for naturalising in an 'old meadow' or for trailing in a sunny hedge-bottom, flowering from late spring through the summer. Like other members of the pea family, it has nodules in its roots which fix nitrogen and increase soil fertility. Easily propagated by dividing the roots in spring or from seed sown in spring where they are to flower. Available from a few nurseries.

The flowers are visited mainly by bumble-bees which are strong enough to force their way between the petals and have tongues long enough to reach the nectar at the bottom of the long flower-tube. They pick up pollen on the way which has been shed before the flowers open. The pods may be invaded by the 'maggots' of tortricoid moths.

Leucanthemum vulgare oxeye daisy

This perennial herb, up to 80cm, is our largest white daisy recognised by yellow-centred heads of florets up to 5cm across at the top of almost hairless, erect, branching stems bearing stalkless, oblong, roughly-toothed leaves which clasp the stem at the base, a contrast to the basal leaves which are spoon-shaped with long stalks.

Oxeye daisies grow in meadows, on roadsides and in other grassy places on moderately acid to calcareous soils throughout Scotland from sea-level to 450m in the Highlands.

A showy, long-flowering summer plant for herbaceous borders or for naturalising in a wild meadow area from which the young leaves can be gathered to add to salads or sandwiches – in moderation as the taste is strong: the flower-heads can be used like dandelions for wine-making. Best propagated by division in spring or autumn but also easily raised from seed. Widely available from nurseries, but choose small-headed native forms.

An important wildlife plant for a great variety of butterflies and moths, bees, wasps, beetles, soldier- and hover-flies. Also inhabited by the caterpillars of tortricoid moths which first mine the leaves but later fold them together to create shelters.

Ligusticum scoticum Scots lovage

A hairless, bright-green perennial, up to 90cm, readily recognised by its leaves divided into three and then into three again to produce nine lobes, coarsely toothed in the upper half. The greenish-white flowers are

arranged in umbels and develop narrow egg-shaped fruits, up to 7mm long, with prominent ridges.

Scots lovage is found all round the coast of Scotland where it grows on cliffs and rocks only a few metres from the sea and out of the reach of grazing sheep.

An interesting plant which might be grown in the herb garden along with other members of the carrot family like fennel, parsley and ordinary lovage. The leaves were eaten as a pot-herb and sheep clearly find them tasty: the root is aromatic and pungent. Best propagated from seed and planted out 30cm apart in good garden soil. Available from a few nurseries.

Like other umbels, Scots lovage is mainly pollinated by crawling flies, thrips, beetles and short-tongued bees attracted to the nectar at the base of the tiny flowers.

Linaria vulgaris common toadflax

A striking perennial, spreading freely by a creeping underground rhizome, with upright stems rising to 60cm, and upright leaves,

narrow and greyish-green, resembling the 'flax' in its name. Stems terminate in spikes of yellow and orange antirrhinum-like flowers, up to 3cm long with straight spurs, which appear from July onwards and develop into round capsules.

Common toadflax is only truly common on river shingle, railway banks, roadsides and waste places. It is found in the lowlands of south and east Scotland as far north as the Moray Firth, but is otherwise very scattered and absent from the northern isles.

A brilliant flower for the herbaceous border, so long as it can be prevented from spreading, or for a dry bank or sunny hedge-bottom. An essence of fresh material is used in homeopathy for treating diarrhoea and cystitis. Easily propagated by division in spring or autumn. Available from several nurseries where a curious 'peloric' form, with each flower having five spurs, may be found.

An important bee flower with the spurs full of nectar produced at the base of the ovary, which can be reached only by long-tongued bees guided by a smooth channel c.1mm wide between two orange, hairy ridges on the lower side of the flower tube.

Lotus corniculatus common bird's-foot-trefoil

A hairless, creeping perennial, recognised by having five, not three, leaflets, the lower pair attached to the solid stem. The large pea-like, yellow flowers, which appear in summer, are arranged in groups of four to five at the tip of the stem and develop into pods spread out like a bird's foot.

Common bird's-foot-trefoil is found in sand dunes, grassland and heaths on acid to basic free-draining soils from sea-level to 900m in the Highlands.

Although tolerant of a wide range of conditions, it is best used to naturalise in a meadow area or in a dry sunny hedge-bottom. Also called 'bacon-and-eggs' after the red streaks which may be seen on the

petals of some forms. Propagated by division of clumps in spring or from seeds which should be scarified before sowing in autumn. Available from several nurseries but make sure you buy native Scottish stock with pods less than 20mm long.

The nectar of the flowers is high in sugar and attracts butterflies, bumble- and honey-bees, and solitary wasps which 'rob' the flowers by biting through the base of the petals. Leaves are eaten by the caterpillars of common blue, dingy skipper and green hairstreak butterflies.

Lychnis alpina alpine catchfly

A tufted, perennial herb with basal rosettes of short, stalkless, oblong leaves up to 5cm from amongst which arise leafy, hairless flowering stems up to 15cm tall. These terminate in a crowded cluster of rose-coloured flowers of five deeply-divided petals which develop into small, round capsules opening by five turned-down teeth.

Alpine catchfly is a very rare mountain plant limited to a few places in Angus where it grows on bare rock with a high content of heavy metals at c.870m.

A very attractive plant for the rock garden, completely frost and drought resistant, though benefiting from a richer soil than

most other species of *Lychnis*. The name *Lychnis* comes from the Greek *Lychnos*, a lamp, referring to the brightly coloured flowers. Easily propagated from seed sown in the open in March. Widely available from nurseries.

Visited by butterflies attracted by the 'lamp' to the nectar but, if because of bad weather, they do not catch 'butter-' or other 'flies', the flowers are automatically self-pollinated.

Lychnis flos-cuculi ragged-Robin

A tall, reddish-stemmed perennial up to 80cm with pairs of narrow, opposite leaves. It is immediately recognised by its 'ragged' flowers which seem to be made of 20 rose-red

petals but are the basic five of the pink family each cut into four thin lobes. The flowers develop a broad, oval capsule opening by five turned-down teeth.

Ragged-Robin is widespread in moderately acid to calcareous soils in damp woods and marshes, on river banks and loch margins throughout lowland Scotland but ascending to over 600m in Atholl.

Extremely attractive in a marshy corner or at the edge of a garden pond with colourful stems and flowers: the white form would excel against a dark background. *Flos-cuculi* is Latin for cuckoo-flower, alluding to its coming into flower when the cuckoo sings in May. The red and white forms are both widely available from nurseries.

Attracts nectar-seeking butterflies such as the green-veined white, and hover-flies, whilst caterpillars of the campion moth feed on the ripening seeds from July to September.

Lychnis viscaria sticky catchfly

A tufted perennial up to 60cm, woody at the base. Its dark-green or purple stems are very sticky beneath each pair of long, narrow leaves, and terminate in a spike of flowers in whorls. Each flower has five purplish-red, slightly notched petals and develops into an oval capsule opening by five spreading teeth. Sticky catchfly is a rare species on cliffs and dry rocks of volcanic origin in south and east Scotland and north to Perthshire, where it ascends to over 400m in Rannoch.

A handsome and very hardy plant for a dry, sunny border or a corner of the rock garden coming into flower in June. Readily raised from seed sown in March in the open, or by division in the autumn. Available from several nurseries, including a white variety, but avoid the 'pleno' forms which, lacking nectar, are less valuable for insects.

The normal flowers are good sources of nectar for butterflies and long-tongued bumble-bees. The sticky stems and flower-stalks are like living fly-papers, trapping ants and other small insects before they can reach the nectar.

Lysimachia nummularia creeping-Jenny

Familiar to gardeners and readily recognised by its long, trailing stems with pairs of rounded, 2p-sized leaves on opposite sides, and by its bright-yellow, bowl-shaped, 5-petalled flowers at the end of short stalks

rising from the base of the leaves. It very rarely produces ripe fruit.

A rare plant in Scotland where, as a native, it is only found in a few lowland hedgerows, ditches and meadows in the south, reaching its northern limit in Fife.

A useful summer-flowering plant for damp and slightly shady areas or pond margins where it provides good ground cover, and for hanging baskets or pots. The golden-leaved form 'aurea' may be preferred for darker corners. An infusion of fresh stems may be taken as a remedy for various internal disorders. The leaf-shape has been responsible for other common names such as 'herb twopence' or 'moneywort'. Easily propagated by division in spring or autumn and widely available from nurseries along with the 'aurea' form.

The flowers produce no nectar but are full of pollen which attracts bees and other pollen eating insects.

Lysimachia vulgaris yellow loosestrife

A tall, hairy perennial up to 1.5m, spreading by underground stems. It has lance-shaped leaves in whorls of two to four, and a long spike of yellow, 5-petalled flowers, up to 1.5cm across, on short stalks, which develop into globe-shaped capsules splitting longitudinally.

A lowland species found in tall herb vegetation in marshes, on river banks and along loch margins, where cattle cannot

reach, and in scattered places through the southern half of Scotland reaching north to Argyll.

Yellow loosestrife is a handsome, strong-growing species ideal for the edge of a garden pond, along a stream or for naturalising in a damp hollow, and is tolerant of some shade. Recommended by the 17th century herbalist Nicholas Culpeper for stopping nose-bleeds and tummy upsets. Best propagated by division of plants in spring and autumn. Widely available for nurseries.

The flowers are nectarless and scentless but several species of wasp and a tiny solitary bee, *Macropis labiata*, are attracted to the abundant pollen: the females of the bee leave their own scent which then attracts other females and, more especially, males.

Myosotis sylvatica
wood forget-me-not

The most widely cultivated of our wild forget-me-nots, this hairy biennial or perennial is instantly recognised by its terminal spikes of large, wheel-shaped blue flowers with orange centres, up to 1cm across with styles, longer than the calyx tube, clearly visible when viewed from the side after the petals have fallen.

Found in damp, lowland woods, mainly in SE Scotland but also frequent, and possibly native, on river banks on the south side of the Moray Firth. It also occurs widely as an escape from gardens.

Despite its tendency to wander, wood forget-me-not is a faithful and persistent species for edging the front of the border or for naturalising in a damp wooded corner, though here the white-flowered form 'alba' may be preferred. *Myosotis* comes from the Greek and means 'mouse-ear' which refers to the shape and hairiness of the leaves. Known world-wide as 'forget-me-not' – in France as 'ne m'oubliez pas' and in Germany as 'vergissmeinnicht'. It is best propagated from seed sown in spring and planted out in October. The white form may be available from some nurseries.

The nectar at the base of the tubular flowers attracts butterflies, long-headed flies and bee-flies but, if pollinators do not visit the flowers, they are usually self-pollinated.

Nymphaea alba white water-lily

When in bloom the large, white, many-petalled flowers floating on the surface are unmistakable. When there are only round leaves one must look at the amount they are divided to separate white from yellow water-lilies: split almost to halfway in the white but only one third of the way in the yellow. After flowering, fruits of the white sink below the surface, in the yellow they rise above it.

White water-lilies are found in slow-moving streams, ponds and lochs throughout lowland Scotland though rising to over 400m in the Highlands. Particularly abundant in the west and in the Outer Hebrides where a

small-flowered form occurs in lochs poor in nutrients.

The white water-lily makes a brilliant display in a garden pond in summer, though flowers submerge at night. Best planted in plastic baskets lined with sacking and filled with a rich compost and sunk up to 1.5m deep. The underwater stems are sometimes eaten in northern Europe whilst, in the past, they were commended as a cure for baldness. Propagated by dividing the thick rhizome in March and April. Available from most nurseries: the small-flowered form may be sold as subsp. *occidentalis.*

The flowers, which produce curious boron-containing nectar, are fragrant when first open and attract bees, flies and beetles to assist in pollination.

Pilosella officinarum mouse-ear-hawkweed

A low-growing perennial which produces long, white runners bearing small, distant leaves and terminating in an overwintering rosette of leaves which are rounded, broadest near the tip, dark-green above but white-felted beneath. In summer leafless flower-stalks carry solitary heads of pale-yellow florets, the outer ones red-striped beneath.

Mouse-ear hawkweed grows in short grassland, on heaths, dry banks and rocks, both acid and alkaline, throughout Scotland, except Shetland, rising to 900m in the Highlands.

An enchanting little plant for the rock garden, a dry sunny bank or trailing over a wall. 'Mouse-ear' is a reference to the shape and hairiness of the leaves which, if picked and made into an infusion, can be used for the treatment of enteritis, influenza and cystitis. Easily propagated by division at almost any season. Available from a number of nurseries.

Mouse-ear hawkweed is a small wild-life haven with the florets producing abundant pollen, which attracts pollen-eating beetles, and nectar which is reached by butterflies, bumble-bees, bee-flies and hover-flies. The leaves may be host to a gall-wasp which produces swellings on the mid -rib.

Potentilla crantzii alpine cinquefoil

A prostrate perennial producing short, ascending branches bearing palm-shaped leaves with five toothed leaflets and with flowering stems in their axils. The flowers are large, up to 2.5cm across, with five deep-yellow, notched petals, often with a darker orange spot near the base.

Alpine cinquefoil grows on rock ledges, occasionally in grassland, usually base-rich, in the mountains of Scotland, mainly in the Highlands where it ascends to over 1000m, but also with scattered localities in the Southern Uplands and the far north.

A handsome plant for the rock garden or the alpine house, coming into flower in May and requiring a free-draining soil in a sunny position. Readily propagated by the division of the roots and planting out in spring or autumn, or may be raised from seed sown under glass in March. Widely available from nurseries.

Nectar is secreted by a ring at the base of the petals and attracts pollinating insects such as bees and wasps. Pollination is necessary to stimulate production of seed, though the majority are produced apomictically - the ovum is not fertilised by a male nucleus.

Primula scotica Scottish primrose

Similar to bird's-eye primrose, P. *farinosa*, but found nowhere else in the world, this perennial has rosettes of leaves, broadest near the tip and with no teeth on the margin and hairless above but white and floury beneath. Short flowering stems, rarely over 10cm, arise from the centre and terminate in a cluster of purple flowers, with five notched,

overlapping or contiguous petals, developing into small, egg-shaped capsules longer than the calyx with five erect teeth.

Found only in damp pastures, often near the sea on exposed cliff-tops, in Sutherland, Caithness and Orkney where it is often locally abundant. The nearest related species, *P. scandinavica*, is in Norway.

Scottish primrose need not be grown only for patriotic reasons: it is a beautiful, compact species with rich flower colour and attractive leaves, to be tried with other alpines where it will need an open gritty loam. Propagation is by division of the plants as soon as flowering is over in late summer or by raising from seed sown in a cold frame when it ripens. Available from numerous nurseries.

Most primroses are heterostylous (having styles of two different lengths to ensure cross-pollination by bees, butterflies and moths), but in *P. scotica* they are all the same length (homostylous) and probably self-fertile, a safeguard against the absence of pollinators in the exposed and isolated areas it grows in.

Primula veris cowslip

In leaf it is difficult to separate cowslip from primrose though they narrow more abruptly into the leaf stalk, but in flower it is easily recognised by its bare, shortly hairy, flowering stalks, up to 20cm, terminating in a cluster of nodding, deep-yellow, tubular flowers with five petals much shorter than those of primrose and strongly curved

inwards. The flowers develop into an egg-shaped capsule enclosed in the enlarged calyx.

Cowslips are scattered in base-rich grassland throughout the lowlands of the south and east of Scotland and in a few places on the west coast as well as in Orkney.

One of our most delightful spring flowers ideal for naturalising in a meadow on a neutral or alkaline soil – once established it will spread of its own accord. The name cowslip is a polite form of cowslop or cowpat, in reference to the way it grows in scattered clumps in grassland, and a better one for labelling the delicate wine which can be made from the flowers gathered in May and June. Readily raised from seed sown in pans in a cold frame. Widely available from nurseries.

The long tubular flowers are a useful source of nectar and attract bee-flies, solitary bees and butterflies and moths which effect the pollination of this heterostylous species.

Primula vulgaris primrose

The crinkly leaves narrow gradually into the leaf-stalk from which the familiar, hairy stalked, flowers first arise in spring and continue well into summer. The large flowers, up to 4cm across, are heterostylous – some plants have flowers with the style above the stamens (pin-eyed) and others have the

style below (thrum-eyed). The flowers develop into capsules full of sticky seeds.

Primroses grow in woodlands or on shady banks, and also in open grassland, especially near the coast, on moderately acid to base-rich soils throughout Scotland, ascending to about 600m in Atholl.

A familiar garden plant which can be used for bedding or for naturalising in a damp, shady corner. It might be mixed with the very attractive cowslip primrose hybrid, *P. veris* × *vulgaris*, with flowers clustered like a cowslip but the size and colour of a primrose: it grows wild along the east coast. Readily propagated by division in spring and autumn, or raised from seed sown in pans in a cold frame in autumn. Widely available from nurseries.

The nectar at the bottom of the long flower tube is food for butterflies, moths, solitary bees, hover-flies and, particularly, bee-flies. The sticky seeds attract ants which carry them away, so dispersing them.

Prunella vulgaris selfheal

A creeping perennial spreading by short, rooting runners, with square stems terminating in cylindrical clusters of violet flowers with pairs of oval leaves, usually with untoothed margins, beneath them. After flowering the purple-tinged, two-lipped calyx closes up and persists.

Selfheal is one of the commonest plants of grassland, heath and scrub, growing throughout Scotland on moderately acid to base-rich soils from coastal dunes to over 700m in the Breadalbane Mountains of Perthshire.

Too vigorous and successful for the flower bed, but it is ideal for naturalising in grassland in the open or in the light shade of a shrubbery or orchard, where it will give large patches of colour in flower and in fruit from June onwards. It may also be gathered and mixed with other wild plants and used as a vegetable in soups and stews but its value as a cure for the throat infection, Brunella, after which it was named, is doubtful. Readily propagated by division in spring or autumn. Widely available from nurseries where a white form may also be found.

A ring of hairs in the throat of the flowers prevents small insects from stealing the nectar without pollinating them – this is mainly done by bees.

Ranunculus lingua greater spearwort

A tall perennial herb, up to 1.2m, recognised by its long, narrow, spear-like leaves which have a bluish patina. From June to September its hollow stems bear large, yellow, 'buttercup' flowers, up to 5cm across, on hairy but unforrowed stalks.

Greater spearwort grows in marshes and tall herb vegetation at the edge of pools and lochs where the water is neutral to alkaline. It is found in a few scattered localities in south and east Scotland but is declining through drainage.

A handsome species to introduce to the margin of a pond where its attractive leaves and golden flowers will delight throughout the summer - but do not plant where cattle can reach as the sap is poisonous. Readily propagated by dividing the stout underground stems and planting out in spring. Widely available from nurseries: the large-flowered form 'grandiflorus' being particularly recommended.

Mainly cross-pollinated by insects attracted to the nectar and pollen including butterflies, moths, thrips, hover-flies, fever-flies, bees and small beetles. May also be self-pollinated by rain when pollen floats over the surface of water-filled flowers to receptive stamens.

Rosa pimpinellifolia burnet rose

A low-growing deciduous shrub with erect stems, rarely exceeding 40cm, armed with a mixture of straight prickles and stiff bristles. It spreads by suckers and often grows in large patches. In June and July the bushes are covered in white or pinkish flowers which produce hips, differing from all other native roses by being black not red.

Burnet rose is scattered throughout lowland Scotland: though rising to 500m in the east it is most abundant near the coast and is a feature of sand dunes and sandy heaths everywhere except the northern isles.

Forms very attractive patches of colour of both flower and fruit but it can be difficult to control if it invades the rock garden. Both Latin and English names refer to the resemblance of the leaves to those of burnet-saxifrage, *Pimpinella saxifraga*, a member of the carrot family. Easily propagated by separating the suckers in autumn. Widely available from nurseries but avoid the double forms.

The flowers do not contain much nectar but are visited and pollinated by bees, beetles and thrips which seek the pollen. The leaf stalks and mid-rib are attacked by gall-wasps producing spherical swellings whilst the leaves may be mined by the larvae of small moths.

Scutellaria galericulata skullcap

A hairy perennial belonging to the mint family with square stems up to 50cm, carrying pairs of toothed, pointed leaves. Recognised by its bright blue flowers, arranged in pairs, pointing in the same direction and with their petals forming a tube much longer than the calyx. The calyx has a large leafy flange on the top said to resemble a galerum, a Roman helmet-like skullcap. *Scutellaria* also describes the calyx – a scutella is a saucer or dish – an upside-down skullcap?

Skullcap is scattered throughout the lowlands of Scotland except for the north-east and the northern isles, and is particularly abundant in the west where it grows in moderately acid to base-rich soils on the edges of ponds and streams, in marshes and on boulder beaches. A valuable and not too vigorous species for the margin of a garden pond or for naturalising in a marshy hollow. An infusion taken two or three times a day may be tried to cure throat infections. Propagated from seed

sown out-of-doors in April or by division of the roots in spring. Available from several nurseries.

The two lateral petals form a bulge in the mouth of the flower which ensures that even small visiting insects are covered in the pollen which the anthers shower down from above.

Sedum acre biting stonecrop

A hairless, evergreen, creeping and mat-forming perennial rarely exceeding 10cm with overlapping, triangular, fleshy leaves which are hot and acrid to the taste. The bright yellow flowers, c.12mm across, which cover the whole plant in June and July, are carried on two to three main branches with two to four flowers at each fork.

Biting stonecrop is widespread on walls, roofs, rocks and shingle and in sand dunes, especially if they are base-rich, throughout lowland Scotland though it is absent from Shetland as a native.

A splendid species for dry walls, edging the rock garden or for covering a bank or old roof. Another English name, wall-pepper, aptly describes its habitat and taste and, though recommended in the past as a cure for ulcers and fevers, it cannot have been pleasant medicine to take. Readily propagated by division between November and April. Available from a few nurseries: the var. *aureum* with bright gold stems and leaf tips in spring may be preferred.

The flowers are full of nectar which is easily reached and attracts ichneumon wasps, which also take the pollen. Perhaps not surprisingly the acrid leaves are not eaten by caterpillars.

Sedum rosea roseroot

Hairless stems, carrying roundish, fleshy leaves, toothed at the top, rise to c.30cm from a very thick, scaly rootstock. Male and female flowers are on separate plants, clustered at the top of the stems, and have four greenish-yellow petals. The male is longer than the sepals, the female the same length, and develop in the latter into four erect 'pods', which become orange when ripe.

Roseroot grows on mountain rocks throughout most of the Highlands ascending to 1175m on the Breadalbane Mountains of Perthshire but is also widespread in the west at low levels especially on sea cliffs from the Mull of Galloway to the tip of Unst in Shetland: there are a few localities on the east coast.

A very desirable plant for the rock garden giving colour from attractive leaves, flowers and fruits from late spring to early autumn. Named 'roseroot' because when the root is cut or bruised it gives off a rose-like smell. Readily propagated by division in autumn, which is the best way to ensure having both

male and female plants. Widely available from nurseries.

Even though the nectar is partially concealed, it can be reached by short-tongued insects such as midges and small flies. Visiting insects are essential to carry pollen from male to female plants.

Silene dioica red campion

One of our most attractive perennial flowers instantly recognised by the masses of deep-pink, deeply-lobed, 5-petalled flowers carried on purple stems up to 80cm tall, with broad leaves in opposite pairs. Red campion is dioecious, having separate male and female plants: female flowers have a fatter calyx than males, and enclose a capsule which develops with ten turned down teeth.

Red campion can be found in oak and birch woods, on sea cliffs, and on mountain screes and ledges on acid to neutral soils throughout Scotland, rising to 900m on Lochnagar, but is rare in the north-west and Outer Hebrides.

A wonderful plant for the middle of the border or for naturalising in a hedge-bottom or wooded corner. There is a coastal-cliff form, with deep magenta flowers on more robust, hairier stems, which is even more attractive and which, like other forms, can be readily raised from seed sown in spring in pans placed in cold frames and planted out in autumn. Widely available from nurseries.

The nectar at the bottom of the long, tubular flowers can be reached by butterflies, long-tongued bumble-bees and hover-flies. The leaves are food for caterpillars of lychnis and marbled coronet moths.

Silene uniflora sea campion

A low, cushion-forming perennial, up to 20cm, recognised by its hairless, bluish-green stems and opposite leaves and, in mid-summer, by the profusion of white flowers with five deeply-cleft petals surrounded below by a thin-walled, net-veined, pale-green calyx which later hides the developing, globe-shaped, seed capsule.

Sea campion not only grows on shingle or pebble beaches and on sea-cliffs all round the coast of Scotland and on most of the remotest islands, but also ascends to nearly 1000m in the Highlands where it is found on cliff-ledges, loch margins and stream banks.

An excellent low-growing, floriferous species for the front of a rocky border or for allowing to trail over the edge of a gravel path. Closely related to bladder campion, *S. vulgaris*, and, if they are grown together, hybridisation may occur. Easily propagated by division and

immediate replanting in spring in pans placed in a cold frame. Widely available from nurseries.

Both the nectar at the bottom of the flower and the scent attract pollinating long-tongued bees and night-flying moths, but bumble-bees may bite through the base of the flower and take nectar without touching the pollen. The capsules are often inhabited by seed-eating caterpillars.

Solanum dulcamara bittersweet

A member of the potato family with long straggling stems, with which it can climb several metres in bushes, and potato-like leaves with a large terminal lobe and several smaller leaflets below. The dramatic flowers, which appear in June, have five reflexed, purple petals and a cone of bright-yellow anthers at the centre which develop into small, round, red berries.

Bittersweet is scattered in hedges, wet woodlands and on shingle beaches through the lowlands of south and east Scotland, with only a few coastal localities in the west. It is totally absent, as a native, from the outer isles.

A useful plant to train up a trellis or to naturalise in a hedge where the flowers and fruits will give colour well into the autumn, but keep children away from the berries because they are mildly poisonous. The young stems contain a toxic alkaloid, solanine, bitter to the taste at first and then sweet, hence the English name. Best

propagated by taking soft or semi-hard cuttings of short side shoots in summer. Available from some nurseries.

A specialised pollen flower attracting bees which cause the pollen to be released from holes at the tips of the anthers by rapidly vibrating their wings as they hang from the anther cone.

Solidago virgaurea goldenrod

A late-summer flowering perennial, up to 75cm, instantly recognised by its branched spikes of golden-yellow, daisy-like flowers at the top of erect stems bearing alternating, oval, hairless leaves, usually with a toothed margin.

Goldenrod is widespread on acid to neutral soils throughout Scotland from sea-shore sand dunes and lowland woods and hedgebanks to mountain ledges at over 1100m in the Highlands where a compact form, var. *cambrica*, up to only 20cm with unbranched 'rods', is found.

This compact form is excellent for the rock garden whilst taller forms make a brave display in the herbaceous border against a dark background. 'Solidago' comes from the

Latin *solidare*, to make whole, referring to its alleged value in healing wounds either as an ointment or as an infusion drunk hot. Easily propagated by division of the clumps in spring or autumn. Available from a number of nurseries but var. *cambrica* only rarely.

Visited by several species of nectar-seeking bees, solitary wasps and short-tongued flies as well as by less selective beetles which eat the pollen and anthers and lick up all the nectar. Mountain forms, particularly, are automatically self-pollinated.

Stellaria holostea greater stitchwort

A creeping, spring-flowering, straggling perennial with weak stems bearing pairs of narrow, pointed leaves with rough margins, from which arise, to 60cm, branched, lax inflorescences of large white flowers up to 3cm across with deeply 2-lobed petals. These develop into globe-shaped capsules as long as the calyx and contain reddish-brown, kidney-shaped seeds.

Greater stitchwort grows in woods and hedgebanks, and on rocky shores on mildly acid to calcareous soils throughout most of Scotland but is absent from most of the mountains above 650m and from the outer isles.

With its masses of white flowers, it is a useful plant for a shady corner or hedge-bottom. May also assist over-enthusiastic gardeners suffering from 'stitch' as it was formerly commended as a remedy for that complaint – mixed with wine and powdered acorns. Propagated by division in spring or autumn and by raising from seed sown in pans in autumn. Available from a number of nurseries.

Visited for its pollen and partially concealed nectar by a wide range of insects including many butterflies and moths, bees, hoverflies, bee-flies and beetles. The leaves provide food for the caterpillars of various dart and yellow underwing moths.

Succisa pratensis devil's-bit scabious

A low-growing, sparsely-hairy perennial, up to 80cm, differing from other scabiouses by having all its leaves undivided and the majority in a rosette at the base. The florets, in compact heads, are 4-lobed and deep purplish blue. Some plants, with smaller heads, have only female florets whilst in others, with larger ones, they are hermaphrodite.

Devil's-bit scabious is common and widespread on acid to neutral soils throughout Scotland in marshes, fens, wet meadows and damp woods from sea level to

over 800m in the Breadalbane Mountains of Perthshire.

A compact, not-too vigorous species ideal for naturalising in a damp meadow or round the margin of a pond where it can provide an intense blue sheen in late summer. Called 'Devil's-bit' because the root-stock is abruptly shortened, bitten off by the devil furious at the plant's success as a 'cure-all', but best used today only for gargling with an infusion made from the dried plant. Propagated by division in spring or autumn. Widely available from nurseries.

Very important for insects: the nectar attracts masses of late flying butterflies like the red admiral, as well as mining bees and hover-flies, whilst the leaves are enjoyed by the caterpillars of marsh fritillaries and narrow-bordered bee hawk-moths.

Symphytum tuberosum
tuberous comfrey

A spreading perennial, with knotted underground 'tubers' and unbranched stems, up to 50cm, bearing alternate oval leaves up to 15cm long, the largest in the middle of the stem, and without wings on the leaf-stalk which run down the stem as in our other native comfrey, *S. officinale*. The drooping yellow, tubular flowers have a calyx with deeply cut lobes three times as long as the tube below.

Tuberous comfrey grows in moist woods, on woodland margins, hedge- and river-banks throughout the lowlands of south and east Scotland north to Caithness.

An excellent summer-flowering species for the middle of the herbaceous border or for naturalising in a woodland corner. Not as palatable as common comfrey but once grown as food for animals though its nutritional value is not very high. Best propagated by dividing the tubers in spring. Available from a number of nurseries.

The nectar at the bottom of the long, tubular flowers can only be reached legitimately by powerful insects like bumble-bees which can push their proboscis past the scales in the throat, but some steal nectar through a hole bitten in the side of the petals.

Thymus polytrichus wild thyme

A low, creeping, mat-forming, woody perennial with square, slender stems, hairy on two opposite sides, bearing pairs of small, oval, strongly-veined leaves, giving off a sweet odour when crushed. The stems terminate in tight heads of rose-purple flowers with four equal petals and a 2-lipped calyx.

A common and widespread species of dry grassland, rocks and heaths on acid to base-rich soils from sea-shore sand dunes to over 1100m in the Breadalbane Mountains of Perthshire.

No rock garden, paved area, trough or wall should be without a covering of wild thyme

which will give pleasure to the nose if you walk over it or rub the leaves as you pass, or to the eyes as a rosy splash of colour throughout the summer. Though the thyme of the herb garden is *T. vulgaris* from the Mediterranean, use this milder form in your stuffing instead, it can easily be dried and stored. Best propagated by division in March or April or by raising from seed sown in the spring. Available from nurseries as *T. praecox* subsp *arcticus.*

The flowers are full of nectar which attracts many moths and butterflies, such as the mountain ringlet, bees, solitary wasps and bee-flies. The leaves are eaten by the caterpillars of moths including Ashworth's rustic.

Trifolium medium zigzag clover

Similar to red cover with prominent heads of flowers but distinguished by its zigzag stems, reddish-purple colour, narrower leaflets without a clear V-mark, and long narrow stipules at the base of the leaf-stalk which stand out from the stem.

Zigzag clover is widespread on moderately acid to calcareous soils on grassy banks and by rivers and burns throughout lowland Scotland reaching only 350m in the Highlands, but absent from Shetland.

A handsome clover for a sunny bank or for naturalising in a wild meadow where it will

provide colour from June to September. The young leaves picked before flowering can be added to salads and soups or be eaten on their own cooked like spinach. Rarely available from nurseries and best raised from seed, soaked for 24 hours, before sowing in pans and later pricking out into small pots from which they are planted into the meadow in small groups.

The flowers are full of nectar which attracts many insects especially bees, bee-flies, hover-flies and St Mark's flies. The clustered heads prevent the theft of nectar through the side of the flowers. The leaves are enjoyed by the caterpillars of garden dart and Hebrew character moths.

Trifolium pratense red clover

A sprawling to erect perennial with ascending branches, up to 60cm, recognised by its globe-shaped clusters of flowers, up to 2cm across, and oval leaflets, usually with whitish V-shaped marks in the centre, and by the elliptical stipules at the base of the leaf-stalk ending abruptly in a point c.3mm long. The seed pods, as in other clovers, are hidden by the dead petals.

Red clover grows in grassland on moderately acid to basic soils throughout Scotland from sea-level to 825m in the Highlands.

An important constituent of any wild meadow where the tiny nodules in the roots

help fix nitrogen to enrich the soil so that artificial fertilisers need not be applied. The fresh flower-heads can be made into a potent wine, whilst an infusion of the dried heads makes an excellent tea served with a slice of fresh lemon and sweetened with honey. Rarely available from nurseries but easily raised from seed as for zigzag clover.

The delicate scent of the flowers attracts butterflies and moths and other long-tongued insects, especially bumble- and hive-bees. So valuable is it to these last two that it is sometimes called 'bee-bread'.

Trifolium repens white clover

Our only native, creeping white clover producing rootlets from the nodes on the stem and having trifoliate leaves with a white band encircling the base of each of the three leaflets. The heads of honey-scented flowers are held on long stalks, up to 30cm high, and begin to open in June. The dead flowers remain folded over the drooping 3-4 seeded pods.

White clover grows in grassland on all kinds of soil, acid to calcareous, dry to moist, throughout Scotland from sea-level to 900m in the Highlands.

One of the most useful and floriferous species for the wild meadow where it will thrive if not overshadowed by course grasses

and tall herbs. Also valuable in a lawn where it will stay green in a hot summer when grasses go brown. The young leaves can be gathered before flowering and mixed with a green salad. Readily propagated by taking rooting fragments, potting them up and then planting out in small groups in the meadow, or by raising from seed as for zigzag cover.

Especially important for bee-keepers being amongst the first flowers to produce nectar in bulk after sycamore and dandelion are over. Other visiting insects, like St Mark's flies, are seeking pollen.

Trollius europaeus globeflower

An erect perennial, up to 60cm, with palm-shaped leaves divided into three to five segments and recognised from a distance by the large, shining buttercup flowers up to 3cm across made up of five to 15 golden sepals which surround and hide a similar number of smaller, narrow petals with nectaries at their base. After summer flowering the sepals fall to reveal a cluster of keeled follicles containing shiny, black seeds. Globeflowers grow in damp meadows and open woods, and on rock ledges throughout the Highlands of Scotland to 1000m, but they descend to sea-level in the west and north, though absent from the outer isles.

A wonderful, gay plant for a damp meadow, garden pond margin or beside a rock garden stream, flowering most of the summer. Known also, in Scotland, as locker gowlan, aptly descriptive as 'locker' means locked or closed and a 'gowlan' is a golden flower. Best propagated by division in the autumn and planted in moist loam or raised from seed sown after collection in autumn in pans in a shaded cold frame. Widely available from nurseries.

Visited by numerous small insects seeking the rich production of nectar and pollen. They stay to lay their eggs and the larvae which emerge eat some of the seeds but the rest develop normally.

woodland, with excellent colour from flowers and fruit the summer long. The fruit are edible, though somewhat acid and are best with sugar: without sugar they may be taken as a remedy for diarrhoea. Propagation may be by cuttings of half-ripe shoots taken in summer and raised in a shady frame or from seed sown in a sandy soil in spring. Widely available from nurseries.

Pollinated by hive- and bumble-bees and other long-tongued insects. Caterpillars of white underwing moths and several species of tortricoid moths feed on the leaves, whilst the stems may be swollen after attack by species of fungi.

Vaccinium vitis-idaea cowberry

A low-growing member of the heather family with thick elliptical leaves, very glossy above, pale and gland-dotted beneath, bearing clusters of pinkish-white, bell-shaped flowers from June to August which develop into bright red globular fruits.

Cowberry grows on moorland and in open woodland on acid soils throughout the Scottish Highlands up to over 1100m, but descends to almost sea-level in several areas.

A useful cover plant for a heather or sandstone rock garden or for a peaty

Valeriana officinalis common valerian

A tall perennial, up to 1.5m, with stems, hairy below, carrying opposite pairs of leaves divided into four to five pairs of lanceolate, remotely-toothed leaflets and terminating in a branched inflorescence of clusters of small, pale-pink, tubular flowers with five unequal lobes. These develop into single-seeded nutlets surmounted by a feathery 'parachute' which develops from the calyx and carries the seed away in the wind.

Common valerian grows in tall grassland and bushy places on usually damp, moderately acid to neutral soils throughout Scotland ascending to 700m in the Highlands but is absent from Shetland.

A handsome summer-flowering species for the back of the herbaceous border or for a wild meadow where it will be enjoyed by people and their cats. Cats are attracted to

the curious smell, said to resemble new leather, given off by the roots. Dry roots were formerly placed in the linen cupboard to keep the sheets smelling fresh. Propagation is by division in March or April or by raising from seed sown in a sunny position in a light soil in April. Widely available from nurseries: var. *sambucifolia* is the native Scottish form.

One of the most important insect flowers which will attract masses of butterflies and moths to the garden to feed on its nectar, along with sawflies, bees and wasps and many other, short-tongued, insects which can reach the bottom of the tubular flowers.

Veronica officinalis
heath speedwell

A creeping, rooting, mat-forming perennial with hairy, elliptical, coarsely-toothed, stalkless leaves from the base of which arise, up to 40cm, dense spikes of lilac flowers with 4-lobed petals, the largest above, and two stamens, which develop into flattened 2-valved, hairy pods.

Heath speedwell is found in acid grassland, heaths and open woods throughout Scotland from sea-shore sand dunes to 900m in the Highlands.

A charming addition to a sandstone rock garden or for a sunny hedge-bottom providing a carpet of colour in early summer. *Officinalis* is a Latin word indicating the plant's medicinal value: as a homeopathic ointment it is prescribed as a cure for severe skin conditions, whilst the dried leaves can be added to a herbal tea blend. Easily propagated by taking rooted cuttings in August, growing on in pots and planting out where required the following spring. It can also be raised from seed sown in the open in spring in a light soil. Available from a few nurseries.

A valuable source of nectar which attracts many small pollinating insects including bees, wasps and hover-flies to its small tubular flowers.

Vicia cracca tufted vetch

A scrambling, hairy perennial reaching 2m with the aid of branched tendrils at the end of leaves with six to 15 pairs of narrow leaflets. Spikes of up to 40 blue-purple, pea-like flowers terminate flower stalks, c.10cm

long, which arise from the base of the leaf-stalk from June onwards. Hairless 4–8-seeded pods, up to 2cm long, develop in autumn.

Tufted vetch is found in rough grassland, hedges and other bushy places on moderately acid to calcareous soils throughout Scotland, mainly in the lowlands but reaching 350m in Perthshire.

Our most colourful wild vetch which makes a fine show in late summer trained up a trellis or growing through a hedge, where, if it emerges into an adjacent field, it may be browsed by stock. Has several other names in Scotland including cat-peas, wild fetches and, in Shetland, blue girse. Best propagated by division in spring or autumn or by raising from seed, soaked for 24 hours before sowing in pans, and later planting out where they are wanted. Occasionally available from nurseries.

The flowers, full of nectar, attract pollinating bees which pick up pollen from a 'brush' on the side of the bent style just below the tip where it has been placed by anthers which burst before the flowers open. The leaves are fed on by the caterpillars of several species of tortricoid moths.

Viola riviniana common dog-violet

All violets are recognised by their distinctive heart-shaped leaves and flowers with five unequal petals with an upwardly directed pair above, a lateral pair and a lower, broader one elongating into a spur behind. In common dog-violet this spur is pale, never darker than the petals and, in fruit, the five sepals develop large, backwardly pointing appendages.

This violet occurs very widely in Scotland in pine, birch and oak woods, in scrub, on heaths and rocks and in grassland on acid to calcareous soils from sea-level to over 1000m in the Highlands and is absent only from the wettest habitats.

The best native violet for naturalising in a hedge-bank or woodland garden. The flowers are scentless and the term 'dog' does not mean it is Fido's favourite, rather it refers to its inferiority compared with sweet violet: the same applies to dog's mercury, a useless medicine compared with annual mercury, and to dogwood with berries unfit to eat. Easily propagated by division in late summer or by raising plants from seed sown in a light soil in a cold frame in August or September. Available from several nurseries.

With a lower lip for landing on, and nectar secreted from outgrowths of two stamens which collects at the bottom of the spur, the flowers attract bumble-bees, bee-flies and hover-flies. The leaves are the main food of the caterpillars of pearl-bordered fritillary and small pearl-bordered fritillary butterflies.

Viola tricolor **wild pansy**

Pansies differ from other violets by having the pair of lateral petals directed upwards giving the flowers their characteristic appearance, and by having large, leaf-like stipules at the base of their leaf-stalks. Wild pansies grow to about 15cm producing flowers which are very variable in colour: annual forms are often blue-violet whilst perennials are pure yellow or mixed with blue-violet.

Wild pansies are scattered through Scotland, mainly in the lowlands though ascending to 500m, and grow on acid to base-rich soils in sand dunes, arable fields and short grassland. Flowering in spring and early summer, it is much preferable for the rock garden or sunny bank to the blousey, cultivated garden pansies. The yellow, perennial form, subsp. *curtisii*, native in sea-shore turf, may be preferred. This can be propagated by taking cuttings in late summer and rooting them in a sandy soil in a shaded cold frame. Available from some nurseries, but subsp. curtisii only rarely.

Mainly visited by bumble-bees and other long-tongued insects directed by a yellow spot in the centre of the flower which marks the entrance to the spur from which they collect nectar, giving and receiving pollen in the process.

Checklist of
Scotland's Native Flora

Richard Pankhurst
& Chris Preston

CHECKLIST OF SCOTLAND'S
NATIVE FLORA

Latin	Common	Gaelic/Scots
Achillea millefolium	Yarrow	Eàrr-thalmhainn
Achillea ptarmica	Sneezewort	Cruaidh-lus/ *hard heid(s)*
Adoxa moschatellina	Moschatel	Mosgadal
Aethusa cynapium	Fool's Parsley	Peirsill Bhrèige
Agrimonia eupatoria	Agrimony	Geur-bhileach
Agrimonia procera	Fragrant Agrimony	Geur-bhileach Chùbhraidh
Agrostis canina	Velvet Bent	Fioran Mìn
Agrostis capillaris	Common Bent	Freothainn
Agrostis gigantea	Black Bent	Fioran Dubh
Agrostis stolonifera	Creeping Bent	Fioran
Agrostis vinealis	Brown Bent	Fioran Badanach
Aira caryophyllea	Silver Hair-grass	Sìdh-fheur
Aira praecox	Early Hair-grass	Cuiseag an Earraich
Ajuga pyramidalis	Pyramidal Bugle	Glasair Bheannach
Ajuga reptans	Bugle	Glasair Choille/ *deid man's bellows, dead man's bellows*
Alchemilla alpina	Alpine Lady's-mantle	Trusgan, Meangan Moire
Alchemilla filicaulis	Hairy Lady's-mantle	Fallaing Moire Chaol
Alchemilla glabra	Smooth Lady's-mantle	Fallaing Moire Mhìn
Alchemilla glaucescens		
Alchemilla glomerulans		
Alchemilla wichurae		
Alchemilla xanthochlora	Intermediate Lady's-mantle	Fallaing Moire Bhuidhe
Alisma lanceolatum	Narrow-leaved Water-plantain	
Alisma plantago-aquatica	Water-plantain	Corr-chopag
Alliaria petiolata	Garlic Mustard	Gàirleach Callaid
Allium oleraceum	Field Garlic	Gairleag Achaidh
Allium schoenoprasum	Chives	Saidse
Allium scorodoprasum	Sand Leek	Creamh nan Creag
Allium ursinum	Ramsons	Creamh/ *ramps*
Allium vineale	Wild Onion	Gairleag Moire/ *ingan, sybow, syboe, scallion, sybie*
Alnus glutinosa	Alder	Feàrna/ *aller, alrone, arn*
Alopecurus borealis	Alpine Foxtail	Fiteag Ailpeach
Alopecurus geniculatus	Marsh Foxtail	Fiteag Cham/ *elbow(it) grass*
Alopecurus myosuroides	Black-grass	Fiteag na Machrach
Alopecurus pratensis	Meadow Foxtail	Fiteag an Lòin

Latin	Common	Gaelic/Scots
Ammophila arenaria	Marram	Muran
Anacamptis pyramidalis	Pyramidal Orchid	Mogairlean nan Coilleag
Anagallis arvensis	Scarlet Pimpernel	Falcair
Anagallis minima	Chaffweed	Falcair Mìn
Anagallis tenella	Bog Pimpernel	Falcair Lèana
Anchusa arvensis	Bugloss	Lus Teanga an Daimh
Andromeda polifolia	Bog-rosemary	Ròs Moire Fiadhaich
Anemone nemorosa	Wood Anemone	Flùr na Gaoithe
Angelica sylvestris	Wild Angelica	Lus nam Buadh, Aingealag
Anisantha sterilis	Barren Brome	Bròmas Aimrid
Antennaria dioica	Mountain Everlasting	Spòg Cait
Anthoxanthum odoratum	Sweet Vernal-grass	Borrach
Anthriscus caucalis	Bur Chervil	Costag
Anthriscus sylvestris	Cow Parsley	Costag Fhiadhain
Anthyllis vulneraria	Kidney Vetch	Cas an Uain
Aphanes arvensis	Parsley-piert	Spìonan Moire
Aphanes inexspectata	Slender Parsley-piert	Spìonan Moire Caol
Apium graveolens	Wild Celery	Lus na Smàileig
Apium inundatum	Lesser Marshwort	Fualastar
Apium nodiflorum	Fool's-water-cress	Biolair Brèige
Aquilegia vulgaris	Columbine	Lus a' Chalmain/*columby, grannie's mutch(es)*
Arabidopsis thaliana	Thale Cress	Biolair Thàilianach
Arabis alpina	Alpine Rock-cress	Biolair na Creige Ailpeach
Arabis glabra	Tower Mustard	
Arabis hirsuta	Hairy Rock-cress	Biolair na Creige Ghiobach
Arabis petraea	Northern Rock-cress	Biolair na Creige Thuathach
Arctium minus	Lesser Burdock	Leadan Liosda
Arctostaphylos alpinus	Alpine Bearberry	Grainnseag Dhubh
Arctostaphylos uva-ursi	Bearberry	Grainnseag/*gnashick*
Arenaria norvegica	Arctic Sandwort	
Arenaria serpyllifolia	Thyme-leaved Sandwort	
Armeria maritima	Thrift	Neòinean Cladaich, Tonn a' Chladaich/*sea daisy*
Arnoseris minima	Lamb's Succory	
Arrhenatherum elatius	False Oat-grass	Feur Coirce Brèige/*knot grass, swine('s) arnit*

Latin	Common	Gaelic/Scots
Artemisia absinthium	Wormwood	Burmaid/*wormit*
Artemisia norvegica	Norwegian Mugwort	Gròban Lochlannach
Artemisia vulgaris	Mugwort	Liath-lus/*muggart (kail)*, *muggins*
Arum maculatum	Lords-and-Ladies	Cluas Chaoin
Asplenium adiantum-nigrum	Black Spleenwort	Raineach Uaine
Asplenium marinum	Sea Spleenwort	Raineach na Mara
Asplenium obovatum	Lanceolate Spleenwort	
Asplenium ruta-muraria	Wall-rue	Rù Bhallaidh
Asplenium septentrionale	Forked Spleenwort	Lus a' Chorrain Gòbhlach
Asplenium trichomanes	Maidenhair Spleenwort	Dubh-chasach
Asplenium trichomanes-ramosum	Green Spleenwort	
Aster tripolium	Sea Aster	Neòinean Sàilein
Astragalus alpinus	Alpine Milk-vetch	Bliochd-pheasair Ailpeach
Astragalus danicus	Purple Milk-vetch	Bliochd-pheasair Chorcra
Astragalus glycyphyllos	Wild Liquorice	Bliochd-pheasair Mhìn
Athyrium distentifolium	Alpine Lady-fern	Raineach Moire Ailpeach
Athyrium filix-femina	Lady-fern	Raineach Moire/*leddy bracken, lady bracken, lady fern, leddy fern*
Athyrium flexile	Newman's Lady-fern	
Atriplex glabriuscula	Babington's Orache	Praiseach Mhìn Chladaich
Atriplex laciniata	Frosted Orache	Praiseach Mhìn Airgeadach
Atriplex littoralis	Grass-leaved Orache	Praiseach Mhìn Thràghad
Atriplex longipes	Long-stalked Orache	
Atriplex patula	Common Orache	Praiseach Mhìn Chaol
Atriplex portulacoides	Sea-purslane	Purpaidh
Atriplex praecox	Early Orache	Praiseach Mhìn Thràth
Atriplex prostrata	Spear-leaved Orache	Praiseach Mhìn Leathann
Baldellia ranunculoides	Lesser Water-plantain	Corr-chopag Bheag
Ballota nigra	Black Horehound	Gràbhan Dubh
Barbarea vulgaris	Winter-cress	Treabhach
Bartsia alpina	Alpine Bartsia	Bairtsia Ailpeach

Latin	Common	Gaelic/Scots
Bellis perennis	Daisy	Neòinean/*May gowan, wallie, banwart, gollan, daseyne, May gowan*
Berula erecta	Lesser Water-parsnip	Folachdan Beag
Beta vulgaris	Beet	
Betula nana	Dwarf Birch	Beith Bheag
Betula pendula	Silver Birch	Beith Dhubhach
Betula pubescens	Downy Birch	Beith Charraigeach
Bidens cernua	Nodding Bur-marigold	Sgeachag Moire
Bidens tripartita	Trifid Bur-marigold	Sgeachag Leathann
Blechnum spicant	Hard-fern	Raineach Chruaidh
Blysmus compressus	Flat-sedge	Seisg Rèidh
Blysmus rufus	Saltmarsh Flat-sedge	Seisg Rèisg Ghoirt
Bolboschoenus maritimus	Sea Club-rush	Bròbh
Botrychium lunaria	Moonwort	Lus nam Mìos
Brachypodium pinnatum	Tor-grass	Bròmas Rag
Brachypodium sylvaticum	False Brome	Bròmas Brèige
Brassica nigra	Black Mustard	Sgeallan Dubh
Briza media	Quaking-grass	Conan Cumanta, Crith-fheur, *Conan Cumanta siller shakers, shak-and-trumble, shakie tremlie(s), shaker(s)*
Bromopsis benekenii	Lesser Hairy-brome	
Bromopsis ramosa	Hairy-brome	Bròmas Giobach
Bromus commutatus	Meadow Brome	Bròmas Lòin
Bromus hordeaceus	Common Soft-brome	
Bromus racemosus	Smooth Brome	Bròmas Mìn
Cakile maritima	Sea Rocket	Fearsaideag
Calamagrostis canescens	Purple Small-reed	Cuilc-fheur Corcra
Calamagrostis epigejos	Wood Small-reed	Cuilc-fheur Coille
Calamagrostis purpurea	Scandinavian Small-reed	
Calamagrostis scotica	Scottish Small-reed	Cuilc-fheur Albannach
Calamagrostis stricta	Narrow Small-reed	Cuilc-fheur Beag

Latin	Common	Gaelic/Scots
Callitriche brutia	Pedunculate Water-starwort	
Callitriche hamulata	Intermediate Water-starwort	Biolair Ioc Meadhanach
Callitriche hermaphroditica	Autumnal Water-starwort	Biolair Ioc an Fhoghair
Callitriche obtusangula	Blunt-fruited Water-starwort	Biolair Ioc Eangach
Callitriche platycarpa	Various-leaved Water-starwort	Biolair Ioc Leathann
Callitriche stagnalis	Common Water-starwort	Biolair Ioc
Calluna vulgaris	Heather	Fraoch/*ling, dog heather, hather, heather, dogling*
Caltha palustris	Marsh-marigold	Lus Buidhe Bealltainn *wild fire*
Calystegia sepium	Hedge Bindweed	Dùil Mhial
Calystegia soldanella	Sea Bindweed	Flùr a' Phrionnsa
Campanula glomerata	Clustered Bellflower	Guc Bagaideach
Campanula latifolia	Giant Bellflower	Guc Mòr
Campanula rotundifolia	Harebell	Currac Cuthaige/*gowk's-thimles, thimbles, blaver, thummles, bluebell, blawort, lady's thimbles, leddy's thimbles, harebell*
Capsella bursa-pastoris	Shepherd's-purse	An Sporan/*lady's purse, leddy's purse*
Cardamine amara	Large Bitter-cress	Searbh-bhiolair Mhòr
Cardamine flexuosa	Wavy Bitter-cress	Searbh-bhiolair Chasta
Cardamine hirsuta	Hairy Bitter-cress	Searbh-bhiolair Ghiobach
Cardamine impatiens	Narrow-leaved Bitter-cress	Searbh-bhiolair Chaol
Cardamine pratensis	Cuckooflower	Flùr na Cuthaig/*spink*
Carduus crispus	Welted Thistle	Fòthannan Baltach
Carduus nutans	Musk Thistle	Fòthannan Crom
Carduus tenuiflorus	Slender Thistle	
Carex acuta	Slender Tufted-sedge	Seisg Dhosach Chaol
Carex acutiformis	Lesser Pond-sedge	Seisg Lochain
Carex appropinquata	Fibrous Tussock-sedge	Seisg Shnàithneanach
Carex aquatilis	Water Sedge	Seisg Uisge
Carex arenaria	Sand Sedge	Seisg Ghainmhich
Carex atrata	Black Alpine-sedge	Seisg Ailpeach Dhubh
Carex atrofusca	Scorched Alpine-sedge	Seisg Ailpeach Dhòthach
Carex bigelowii	Stiff Sedge	Dùr-sheisg

Latin	Common	Gaelic/Scots
Carex binervis	Green-ribbed Sedge	Seisg Fhèith-ghuirm
Carex buxbaumii	Club Sedge	Seisg Chuailleach
Carex capillaris	Hair Sedge	Seisg Ghrinn
Carex caryophyllea	Spring-sedge	Seisg an Earraich
Carex chordorrhiza	String Sedge	Seisg Shreangach
Carex curta	White Sedge	Seisg Bhàn
Carex diandra	Lesser Tussock-sedge	Seisg Bhadanach Bheag
Carex dioica	Dioecious Sedge	Seisg Aon-cheannach
Carex distans	Distant Sedge	Seisg Fhada-mach
Carex disticha	Brown Sedge	Seisg Ruadh
Carex divisa	Divided Sedge	Seisg Ghobhlach
Carex divulsa	Grey Sedge	Seisg Liath
Carex echinata	Star Sedge	Seisg Reultach/*bruckles*
Carex elata	Tufted-sedge	Seisg Dhosach
Carex elongata	Elongated Sedge	Seisg Ard
Carex extensa	Long-bracted Sedge	Seisg Anainn
Carex flacca	Glaucous Sedge	Seisg Liath-ghorm
Carex hirta	Hairy Sedge	Seisg Ghiobach
Carex hostiana	Tawny Sedge	Seisg Odhar
Carex lachenalii	Hare's-foot Sedge	Seisg Cas Maighiche
Carex laevigata	Smooth-stalked Sedge	Seisg Mhìn
Carex lasiocarpa	Slender Sedge	Seisg Choilleanta
Carex limosa	Bog-sedge	Seisg na Mòna
Carex magellanica	Tall Bog-sedge	Seisg na Bogaich
Carex maritima	Curved Sedge	Seisg Bheag Dhubh cheannach
Carex microglochin	Bristle Sedge	Seisg Chalgach
Carex muricata	Large-fruited Prickly-sedge	
Carex nigra	Common Sedge	Gainnisg
Carex norvegica	Close-headed Alpine-sedge	Seisg Lochlannach
Carex otrubae	False Fox-sedge	Seisg Gharbh Uaine
Carex ovalis	Oval Sedge	Seisg Ughach
Carex pallescens	Pale Sedge	Seisg Gheal
Carex panicea	Carnation Sedge	Seisg a' Chruithneachd
Carex paniculata	Greater Tussock-sedge	Seisg Bhadanach Mhòr
Carex pauciflora	Few-flowered Sedge	Seisg nan Lusan Gann
Carex pendula	Pendulous Sedge	Seisg Chrom

Latin	Common	Gaelic/Scots
Carex pilulifera	Pill Sedge	Seisg Lùbach
Carex pulicaris	Flea Sedge	Seisg na Deargainn
Carex punctata	Dotted Sedge	Seisg Bhallach
Carex rariflora	Mountain Bog-sedge	Seisg Ailpeach Thearc
Carex recta	Estuarine Sedge	Seisg an Inbhir
Carex remota	Remote Sedge	Seisg Sgarta
Carex riparia	Greater Pond-sedge	Seisg Lochain Mhòr
Carex rostrata	Bottle Sedge	Seisg Shearragach
Carex rupestris	Rock Sedge	Seisg na Creige
Carex saxatilis	Russet Sedge	Seisg Dhonn
Carex spicata	Spiked Sedge	Seisg Spìceach
Carex sylvatica	Wood-sedge	Seisg Choille
Carex vaginata	Sheathed Sedge	Seisg na Truaill
Carex vesicaria	Bladder-sedge	Seisg Bhalganach
Carex viridula	Small-fruited Yellow-sedge	
Carlina vulgaris	Carline Thistle	Cluaran Oir
Carum verticillatum	Whorled Caraway	Carbhaidh Fhàinneach
Catabrosa aquatica	Whorl-grass	Feur-sùghmhor
Catapodium marinum	Sea Fern-grass	
Catapodium rigidum	Fern-grass	
Centaurea nigra	Common Knapweed	Cnapan Dubh/ *horse(s) knot, horse(s) knop, hard heid(s)*
Centaurea scabiosa	Greater Knapweed	Cnapan Dubh Mòr
Centaurium erythraea	Common Centaury	Ceud-bhileach
Centaurium littorale	Seaside Centaury	Dreimire Mara
Centaurium pulchellum	Lesser Centaury	Dreimire Beag
Cephalanthera longifolia	Narrow-leaved Helleborine	Eileabor Geal
Cerastium alpinum	Alpine Mouse-ear	Cluas Luch Ailpeach
Cerastium arcticum	Arctic Mouse-ear	Cluas Luch Artach
Cerastium arvense	Field Mouse-ear	Cluas Luch Achaidh
Cerastium cerastoides	Starwort Mouse-ear	Cluas Luch Reultach
Cerastium diffusum	Sea Mouse-ear	Cluas Luch Mara
Cerastium fontanum	Common Mouse-ear	Cluas Luch Choitcheann
Cerastium glomeratum	Sticky Mouse-ear	Cluas Luch Fhàireagach
Cerastium nigrescens	Shetland Mouse-ear	
Cerastium semidecandrum	Little Mouse-ear	Cluas Luch Bheag
Ceratocapnos claviculata	Climbing Corydalis	Fliodh an Tughaidh

Latin	Common	Gaelic/Scots
Ceratophyllum demersum	Rigid Hornwort	Còrn-lus
Ceterach officinarum	Rustyback	Raineach Ruadh
Chaenorhinum minus	Small Toadflax	Buabh-lìon Beag
Chaerophyllum temulum	Rough Chervil	Costag Ghiobach
Chamerion angustifolium	Rosebay Willowherb	Seileachan Frangach
Chelidonium majus	Greater Celandine	Ceann Ruadh, Aonsgoch
Chenopodium album	Fat-hen	Càl Slapach/*midden weed, melgs*
Chrysanthemum segetum	Corn Marigold	Bile Bhuidhe/*guld, guil, gollan, yellow gowan*
Chrysosplenium alternifolium	Alternate-leaved Golden-saxifrage	Lus nan Laogh Tearc
Chrysosplenium oppositifolium	Opposite-leaved Golden-saxifrage	Lus nan Laogh
Cicerbita alpina	Alpine Blue-sow-thistle	Bliochdan Gorm Ailpeach
Cicuta virosa	Cowbane	Fealladh Bog
Circaea alpina	Alpine Enchanter's-nightshade	Lus na h-Oighe Ailpeach
Circaea lutetiana	Enchanter's-nightshade	Fuinseagach
Cirsium arvense	Creeping Thistle	Fòthannan Achaidh
Cirsium dissectum	Meadow Thistle	
Cirsium heterophyllum	Melancholy Thistle	Cluas an Fhèidh
Cirsium palustre	Marsh Thistle	Cluaran Lèana/*bog th(r)issle*
Cirsium vulgare	Spear Thistle	Cluaran Deilgneach/*burr-thistle, Scotch thistle, Scots thistle*
Cladium mariscus	Great Fen-sedge	Sàbh-sheisg
Clinopodium acinos	Basil Thyme	Lus Mhic an Rìgh
Clinopodium vulgare	Wild Basil	Calaimeilt
Cochlearia anglica	English Scurvygrass	Carran Sasannach
Cochlearia danica	Danish Scurvygrass	Carran Danmhairceach
Cochlearia micacea	Mountain Scurvygrass	Carran an t-Slèibhe
Cochlearia officinalis	Common Scurvygrass	Am Maraiche
Cochlearia pyrenaica	Pyrenean Scurvygrass	
Coeloglossum viride	Frog Orchid	Mogairlean Losgainn
Coincya monensis	Isle-of-Man Cabbage	
Conium maculatum	Hemlock	Iteodha/*hech-how, humlock, scab*
Conopodium majus	Pignut	Cnò-thalmhainn/*arnit, lous(e)y arnut, knotty meal, horneck, earnit*
Convallaria majalis	Lily-of-the-valley	Lili nan Gleann
Convolvulus arvensis	Field Bindweed	Iadh-lus
Corallorrhiza trifida	Coralroot Orchid	Freumh Corail

Latin	Common	Gaelic/Scots
Cornus suecica	Dwarf Cornel	Lus a' Chraois
Coronopus squamatus	Swine-cress	Muic-bhiolair
Corylus avellana	Hazel	Calltainn/*palm (tree), hissel*
Crambe maritima	Sea-kale	Càl na Mara, Morran
Crassula aquatica	Pigmyweed	Luibh Beag Bìodach
Crataegus monogyna	Hawthorn	Sgìtheach/*haw-bush, haw-tree*
Crepis biennis	Rough Hawk's-beard	Lus Curain Garbh
Crepis capillaris	Smooth Hawk's-beard	Lus Curain Mìn
Crepis mollis	Northern Hawk's-beard	Lus Curain Tuathach
Crepis paludosa	Marsh Hawk's-beard	Lus Curain Lèana
Crithmum maritimum	Rock Samphire	Saimbhir/*pasper*
Cruciata laevipes	Crosswort	
Cryptogramma crispa	Parsley Fern	Raineach Pheirsill
Cuscuta epithymum	Dodder	
Cynoglossum germanicum	Green Hound's-tongue	
Cynoglossum officinale	Hound's-tongue	Teanga a' Choin
Cynosurus cristatus	Crested Dog's-tail	Coin-fheur/*kemps, windle strae*
Cystopteris dickieana	Dickie's Bladder-fern	Frith-raineach Dhicianach
Cystopteris fragilis	Brittle Bladder-fern	Frith-raineach
Cystopteris montana	Mountain Bladder-fern	Frith-raineach Beinne
Cytisus scoparius	Broom	Bealaidh/*brume, broom*
Dactylis glomerata	Cock's-foot	Garbh-fheur, Spòg Coilich
Dactylorhiza fuchsii	Common Spotted-orchid	Urach-bhallach
Dactylorhiza incarnata	Early Marsh-orchid	Mogairlean Lèana
Dactylorhiza lapponica	Lapland Marsh-orchid	
Dactylorhiza maculata	Heath Spotted-orchid	Mogairlean Mòintich/*bulldairy, balderry, puddock's spindle, paddock's spindle, paddy's spindle*
Dactylorhiza majalis	Western Marsh-orchid	
Dactylorhiza purpurella	Northern Marsh-orchid	Mogairlean Purpaidh
Dactylorhiza traunsteineri	Narrow-leaved Marsh-orchid	
Danthonia decumbens	Heath-grass	Feur Monaidh
Daucus carota	Wild Carrot	Curran Fiadhain

Latin	Common	Gaelic/Scots
Deschampsia cespitosa	Tufted Hair-grass	
Deschampsia flexuosa	Wavy Hair-grass	Mòin-fheur
Deschampsia setacea	Bog Hair-grass	Mòin-fheur Bogaich
Dianthus deltoides	Maiden Pink	Pinc/*spink*
Diapensia lapponica	Diapensia	Diapainsia
Digitalis purpurea	Foxglove	Lus nam Ban-sìdh/*King's Ellwand, lady's thimbles, leddy's thimbles, witches' paps, thummles, deid man's bells, tod('s) tail(s), bluidy fingers, witch(es')-thimbles, thimbles, dead man's bells*
Diphasiastrum alpinum	Alpine Clubmoss	Garbhag Ailpeach
Diphasiastrum complanatum	Issler's Clubmoss	
Dipsacus fullonum	Wild Teasel	Leadan an Fhùcadair
Draba incana	Hoary Whitlowgrass	Biolradh Gruagain Liath
Draba muralis	Wall Whitlowgrass	
Draba norvegica	Rock Whitlowgrass	Biolradh Gruagain an t-Drosera
intermedia	Oblong-leaved Sundew	Dealt Ruaidhe
Drosera longifolia	Great Sundew	Lus a' Ghadmainn
Drosera rotundifolia	Round-leaved Sundew	Lus na Feàrnaich, Ròs an t-Machall Monaidh
Dryas octopetala	Mountain Avens	
Dryopteris aemula	Hay-scented Buckler-fern	Raineach Phreasach
Dryopteris affinis	Scaly Male-fern	Mearlag
Dryopteris carthusiana	Narrow Buckler-fern	Raineach Chaol
Dryopteris cristata	Crested Buckler-fern	
Dryopteris dilatata	Broad Buckler-fern	Raineach nan Radan
Dryopteris expansa	Northern Buckler-fern	Raineach nan Radan
Dryopteris filix-mas	Male-fern	Marc-raineach
Dryopteris oreades	Mountain Male-fern	
Dryopteris remota	Scaly Buckler-fern	
Dryopteris submontana	Rigid Buckler-fern	

Latin	Common	Gaelic/Scots
Echium vulgare	Viper's-bugloss	Lus na Nathrach
Elatine hexandra	Six-stamened Waterwort	Bosan na Dìge
Elatine hydropiper	Eight-stamened Waterwort	Bosan Teth
Eleocharis acicularis	Needle Spike-rush	Bioran Dealgach
Eleocharis austriaca	Northern Spike-rush	
Eleocharis multicaulis	Many-stalked Spike-rush	Bioran Badanach
Eleocharis palustris	Common Spike-rush	Bioran Coitcheann
Eleocharis quinqueflora	Few-flowered Spike-rush	Bioran nan Lusan Gann
Eleocharis uniglumis	Slender Spike-rush	Bioran Caol
Eleogiton fluitans	Floating Club-rush	Curcais air Bhog
Elymus caninus	Bearded Couch	Taithean
Elytrigia atherica	Sea Couch	
Elytrigia juncea	Sand Couch	Glas-fheur
Elytrigia repens	Common Couch	Feur a' Phuint/*ket, lonnachs, rammock, wreck, string girse, quicken(s), wrack, ronnachs*
Empetrum nigrum	Crowberry	Dearcag Fithich/*crawcrooks, knowperts, heather berry, hillberry, crawberry*
Epilobium alsinifolium	Chickweed Willowherb	Seileachan Fliodhach
Epilobium anagallidifolium	Alpine Willowherb	Seileachan Ailpeach
Epilobium hirsutum	Great Willowherb	Seileachan Mòr
Epilobium montanum	Broad-leaved Willowherb	Seileachan Coitcheann
Epilobium obscurum	Short-fruited Willowherb	Seileachan Fàireagach
Epilobium palustre	Marsh Willowherb	Seileachan Lèana
Epilobium parviflorum	Hoary Willowherb	Seileachan Liath
Epilobium roseum	Pale Willowherb	Seileachan Gasach
Epipactis atrorubens	Dark-red Helleborine	Eileabor Dearg
Epipactis helleborine	Broad-leaved Helleborine	Eileabor Leathann
Epipactis leptochila		
Epipactis palustris	Marsh Helleborine	Eileabor Lèana
Epipactis phyllanthes	Green-flowered Helleborine	
Epipactis youngiana	Young's Helleborine	
Equisetum arvense	Field Horsetail	Earball an Eich
Equisetum fluviatile	Water Horsetail	Clois
Equisetum hyemale	Rough Horsetail	Biorag
Equisetum palustre	Marsh Horsetail	Cuiridin/*paddock pipes, paddy pipes, puddock pipes*

Latin	Common	Gaelic/Scots
Equisetum pratense	Shady Horsetail	Earball an Eich Dubharach
Equisetum sylvaticum	Wood Horsetail	Cuiridin Coille
Equisetum telmateia	Great Horsetail	Earball an Eich Mòr
Equisetum variegatum	Variegated Horsetail	Earball an Eich Caol
Erica cinerea	Bell Heather	Fraoch a' Bhadain/*carline heather, bell hather, bell heather*
Erica tetralix	Cross-leaved Heath	Fraoch Frangach/*bell heather, bell hather*
Erigeron borealis	Alpine Fleabane	Fuath-dheargann Ailpeach
Eriocaulon aquaticum	Pipewort	Pìoban Uisge
Eriophorum angustifolium	Common Cottongrass	Canach/*cannach, bog-cotton, cannach*
Eriophorum latifolium	Broad-leaved Cottongrass	Canach an t-Slèibh
Eriophorum vaginatum	Hare's-tail Cottongrass	Sìoda Monaidh/*cannach, month grass, purlaing, pull ling, canna (down), ling, mosscrop, moss, cat('s) tail(s)*
Erodium cicutarium	Common Stork's-bill	Gob Corra
Erodium lebelii	Sticky Stork's-bill	Gob Corra Leanailteach
Erodium maritimum	Sea Stork's-bill	
Erophila glabrescens	Glabrous Whitlowgrass	Biolradh Gruagain Mìn
Erophila majuscula	Hairy Whitlowgrass	Biolradh Gruagain Giobach
Erophila verna	Common Whitlowgrass	Biolradh Gruagain
Eryngium maritimum	Sea-holly	Cuileann Tràgha
Euonymus europaeus	Spindle	Feòras
Eupatorium cannabinum	Hemp-agrimony	Cainb-uisge
Euphorbia exigua	Dwarf Spurge	Foinne-lus Beag
Euphorbia helioscopia	Sun Spurge	Lus nam Foinneachan/*little guid, little gweedie*
Euphorbia paralias	Sea Spurge	
Euphorbia peplus	Petty Spurge	Lus Leighis
Euphorbia portlandica	Portland Spurge	
Euphrasia anglica	Eyebright	Lus nan Leac
Euphrasia arctica	Eyebright	Lus nan Leac
Euphrasia campbelliae	Eyebright	Lus nan Leac
Euphrasia confusa	Eyebright	Lus nan Leac
Euphrasia foulaensis	Eyebright	Lus nan Leac

Latin	Common	Gaelic/Scots
Euphrasia frigida	Eyebright	Lus nan Leac
Euphrasia heslop-harrisonii	Eyebright	Lus nan Leac
Euphrasia marshallii	Eyebright	Lus nan Leac
Euphrasia micrantha	Eyebright	Lus nan Leac
Euphrasia nemorosa	Eyebright	Lus nan Leac
Euphrasia ostenfeldii	Eyebright	Lus nan Leac
Euphrasia rostkoviana	Eyebright	Lus nan Leac
Euphrasia rotundifolia	Eyebright	Lus nan Leac
Euphrasia scottica	Eyebright	Lus nan Leac
Euphrasia tetraquetra	Eyebright	Lus nan Leac
Fallopia convolvulus	Black-bindweed	Glùineach Dhubh
Festuca altissima	Wood Fescue	Feisd Choille
Festuca arenaria	Rush-leaved Fescue	Feisd Luachrach
Festuca arundinacea	Tall Fescue	Feisd Ard
Festuca filiformis	Fine-leaved Sheep's-fescue	Feur Chaorach Mìn
Festuca gigantea	Giant Fescue	Feisd Mòr
Festuca lemanii	Confused Fescue	
Festuca ovina	Sheep's-fescue	Feur Chaorach
Festuca pratensis	Meadow Fescue	Feisd Lòin
Festuca rubra	Red Fescue	Feisd Ruadh
Festuca vivipara	Viviparous Sheep's-fescue	Feur Chaorach Bèo-breitheach
Filago minima	Small Cudweed	
Filago vulgaris	Common Cudweed	Liath-lus Roid/*son-afore-the-father*
Filipendula ulmaria	Meadowsweet	Cneas Chù Chulainn/ *leddy o the meadow, lady o the meadow, queen of (the) meadow*
Filipendula vulgaris	Dropwort	Greaban
Fragaria vesca	Wild Strawberry	Sùbh-làir Fiadhain
Frangula alnus	Alder Buckthorn	
Fraxinus excelsior	Ash	Uinnseann esh
Fumaria bastardii	Tall Ramping-fumitory	Fuaim an t-Siorraimh Ard

79

Latin	Common	Gaelic/Scots
Fumaria capreolata	White Ramping-fumitory	Fuaim an t-Siorraimh Bàn
Fumaria densiflora	Dense-flowered Fumitory	
Fumaria muralis	Common Ramping-fumitory	Fuaim an t-Siorraimh Coitcheann
Fumaria officinalis	Common Fumitory	Lus Deathach-thalmhainn
Fumaria parviflora	Fine-leaved Fumitory	Lus Deathach-thalmhainn Mìn
Fumaria purpurea	Purple Ramping-fumitory	Fuaim an t-Siorraimh Corcarach
Gagea lutea	Yellow Star-of-Bethlehem	Gaigidhe Buidhe
Galeopsis angustifolia	Red Hemp-nettle	An Gath Corcarach
Galeopsis bifida	Bifid Hemp-nettle	
Galeopsis speciosa	Large-flowered Hemp-nettle	An Gath Mòr
Galeopsis tetrahit	Common Hemp-nettle	Deanntag Lìn, An Gath Dubh
Galium aparine	Cleavers	Garbh-lus/ *guse grass, willie-rin-the-hedge, sticky-Willie, stickers, Robbin-rin-the-hedge, Robbie-rin-the-hedge, grip grass, Robin-roond-the-hedge*
Galium boreale	Northern Bedstraw	Màdar Cruaidh
Galium mollugo	Hedge Bedstraw	
Galium odoratum	Woodruff	Lus a' Chaitheimh
Galium palustre	Common Marsh-bedstraw	Màdar Lèana
Galium saxatile	Heath Bedstraw	Màdar Fraoich
Galium sterneri	Limestone Bedstraw	
Galium uliginosum	Fen Bedstraw	Màdar Uaine
Galium verum	Lady's Bedstraw	Lus an Leasaich, Ruadhain *leddy's beds, lady's beds*
Genista anglica	Petty Whin	Conasg Snàthadach/ *carline spurs, carling spurs*
Genista tinctoria	Dyer's Greenweed	
Gentiana nivalis	Alpine Gentian	Lus a' Chrùbain Sneachda
Gentianella amarella	Autumn Gentian	
Gentianella campestris	Field Gentian	
Geranium columbinum	Long-stalked Crane's-bill	Crobh Preachain Giobach
Geranium dissectum	Cut-leaved Crane's-bill	Crobh Preachain Geàrrte
Geranium lucidum	Shining Crane's-bill	Crobh Preachain Deàlrach

Latin	Common	Gaelic/Scots
Geranium molle	Dove's-foot Crane's-bill	Crobh Preachain Mìn
Geranium pratense	Meadow Crane's-bill	Crobh Preachain an Lòin
Geranium pusillum	Small-flowered Crane's-bill	Crobh Preachain Beag
Geranium robertianum	Herb-Robert	Lus an Ròis, Ruideal
Geranium sanguineum	Bloody Crane's-bill	Creachlach Dearg
Geranium sylvaticum	Wood Crane's-bill	Crobh Preachain Coille
Geum rivale	Water Avens	Machall Uisge
Geum urbanum	Wood Avens	Machall Coille
Glaucium flavum	Yellow Horned-poppy	Barrag Ruadh
Glaux maritima	Sea-milkwort	Lus na Saillteachd
Glechoma hederacea	Ground-ivy	Eidheann Thalmhainn/*grund davy, grund avy*
Glyceria declinata	Small Sweet-grass	Mìlsean Uisge Beag
Glyceria fluitans	Floating Sweet-grass	Mìlsean Uisge
Glyceria maxima	Reed Sweet-grass	
Glyceria notata	Plicate Sweet-grass	Mìlsean Uisge Geugach
Gnaphalium norvegicum	Highland Cudweed	Cnàmh-lus Gàidhealach
Gnaphalium supinum	Dwarf Cudweed	Cnàmh-lus Beag
Gnaphalium sylvaticum	Heath Cudweed	Cnàmh-lus Mòintich
Gnaphalium uliginosum	Marsh Cudweed	Cnàmh-lus Lèana
Goodyera repens	Creeping Lady's-tresses	Mogairlean Ealaidheach
Groenlandia densa	Opposite-leaved Pondweed	Linne-lus dlùth
Gymnadenia conopsea	Fragrant Orchid	Lus Taghte
Gymnocarpium dryopteris	Oak Fern	Sgeamh Dharaich
Gymnocarpium robertianum	Limestone Fern	Raineach Cloich-aoil
Hammarbya paludosa	Bog Orchid	Mogairlean Bogaich
Hedera helix	Common Ivy	Eidheann/*bin(d)wood*
Helianthemum nummularium	Common Rock-rose	Grian-ròs
Helictotrichon pratense	Meadow Oat-grass	Feur Coirce Lòin
Helictotrichon pubescens	Downy Oat-grass	Feur Coirce Clumhach
Heracleum sphondylium	Hogweed	Odharan/*humlock, coo-cakes, kex, bunnel*
Hieracium sabaudum	Savoy Hawkweed	
Hieracium vulgatum	Common Hawkweed	Lus na Seabhaig

Latin	Common	Gaelic/Scots
Hierochloe odorata	Holy-grass	Feur Moire
Hippophae rhamnoides	Sea-buckthorn	Ràmh-dhroigheann Mara
Hippuris vulgaris	Mare's-tail	Earball Capaill
Holcus lanatus	Yorkshire-fog	Feur a' Chinn Bhàin/*hose-grass, windle strae, pluff grass, pyuff gi*
Holcus mollis	Creeping Soft-grass	Mìn-fheur/*pyuff girse, pluff grass*
Honckenya peploides	Sea Sandwort	Lus a' Ghoill
Hordelymus europaeus	Wood Barley	Èorna Coille
Hordeum marinum	Sea Barley	
Hordeum murinum	Wall Barley	Eòrna Luch
Hordeum secalinum	Meadow Barley	Eòrna Lòin
Hornungia petraea	Hutchinsia	
Hottonia palustris	Water-violet	
Huperzia selago	Fir Clubmoss	Garbhag an t-Slèibhe/*fox fit*
Hyacinthoides non-scripta	Bluebell	Bròg na Cuthaig, Fuath- mhuc /*bluebell, wood hyacinth,gowk's hose, craw tae(s)*
Hydrocotyle vulgaris	Marsh Pennywort	Lus na Peighinn
Hymenophyllum tunbrigense	Tunbridge Filmy-fern	Raineach Còinnich Fiaclach
Hymenophyllum wilsonii	Wilson's Filmy-fern	Raineach Còinnich
Hypericum androsaemum	Tutsan	Meas an Tuirc Coille
Hypericum elodes	Marsh St John's-wort	Meas an Tuirc Allta
Hypericum hirsutum	Hairy St John's-wort	Lus an Fhògraidh
Hypericum humifusum	Trailing St John's-wort	Beachnuadh Làir
Hypericum maculatum	Imperforate St John's-wort	Beachnuadh gun Smal
Hypericum perforatum	Perforate St John's-wort	Beachnuadh Boireann
Hypericum pulchrum	Slender St John's-wort	Lus Chaluim Chille
Hypericum tetrapterum	Square-stalked St John's-wort	Beachnuadh Fireann
Hypochaeris glabra	Smooth Cat's-ear	Cluas Cait Mhìn
Hypochaeris radicata	Cat's-ear	Cluas Cait
Ilex aquifolium	Holly	Cuileann/*hollin*
Inula crithmoides	Golden-samphire	
Iris pseudacorus	Yellow Iris	Seileasdair, Sealasdair/*seg, seggan*
Isoetes echinospora	Spring Quillwort	Luibh Cleite an Earraich

Latin	Common	Gaelic/Scots
Isoetes lacustris	Quillwort	Luibh nan Cleiteagan
Isolepis cernua	Slender Club-rush	Curcais Chaol
Isolepis setacea	Bristle Club-rush	Curcais Chalgach
Jasione montana	Sheep's-bit	Putan Gorm/*bluebonnets*
Juncus acutiflorus	Sharp-flowered Rush	Luachair a' Bhlàth Ghèir
Juncus alpinoarticulatus	Alpine Rush	Luachair Ailpeach
Juncus ambiguus	Frog Rush	
Juncus articulatus	Jointed Rush	Lachan nan Damh
Juncus balticus	Baltic Rush	Luachair Bhailtigeach
Juncus biglumis	Two-flowered Rush	Luachair Dà-lus
Juncus bufonius	Toad Rush	Buabh-luachair
Juncus bulbosus	Bulbous Rush	Luachair Bhalgach
Juncus castaneus	Chestnut Rush	Luachair Chastain
Juncus compressus	Round-fruited Rush	Luachair Chruinn
Juncus conglomeratus	Compact Rush	Bròdh-bràighe
Juncus effusus	Soft-rush	Luachair Bhog
Juncus filiformis	Thread Rush	Luachair Shnàthach
Juncus foliosus	Leafy Rush	
Juncus gerardii	Saltmarsh Rush	Luachair Rèisg Ghoirt
Juncus inflexus	Hard Rush	Luachair Chruaidh
Juncus maritimus	Sea Rush	Meithean
Juncus squarrosus	Heath Rush	Brù-chorcan/*stuil-bent*
Juncus subnodulosus	Blunt-flowered Rush	Luachair Gheal
Juncus trifidus	Three-leaved Rush	Luachair Thrì-bhileach
Juncus triglumis	Three-flowered Rush	Luachair Thrì-lusan
Juniperus communis	Common Juniper	*melmot, saving tree, aiten, jenepere, etnach*
Knautia arvensis	Field Scabious	Gille Guirmein/*curl-doddy*
Kobresia simpliciuscula	False Sedge	
Koeleria macrantha	Crested Hair-grass	Cuiseag Dhosach
Koenigia islandica	Iceland-purslane	Cainigidhe

Latin	Common	Gaelic/Scots
Lactuca virosa	Great Lettuce	
Lamiastrum galeobdolon	Yellow Archangel	Deanntag Bhuidhe
Lamium album	White Dead-nettle	Teanga Mhìn
Lamium amplexicaule	Henbit Dead-nettle	Caoch-dheanntag Chearc
Lamium confertum	Northern Dead-nettle	Caoch-dheanntag Thuathach
Lamium hybridum	Cut-leaved Dead-nettle	Caoch-dheanntag Gheàrrte
Lamium purpureum	Red Dead-nettle	Caoch-dheanntag Dhearg
Lapsana communis	Nipplewort	Duilleag-bhràghad
Lathraea squamaria	Toothwort	Slàn-fhiacail
Lathyrus japonicus	Sea Pea	Peasair Tràgha
Lathyrus linifolius	Bitter-vetch	Cairt Leamhna, Carra Meille / *carmele, knapparts*
Lathyrus palustris	Marsh Pea	
Lathyrus pratensis	Meadow Vetchling	Peasair Bhuidhe/ *crow pea, craw pea*
Lathyrus sylvestris	Narrow-leaved Everlasting-pea	
Lavatera arborea	Tree-mallow	
Lemna gibba	Fat Duckweed	Aran Tunnaig
Lemna minor	Common Duckweed	Mac gun Athair
Lemna trisulca	Ivy-leaved Duckweed	Gràn Lachan
Leontodon autumnalis	Autumn Hawkbit	Caisearbhan Coitcheann
Leontodon hispidus	Rough Hawkbit	Caisearbhan Garbh
Leontodon saxatilis	Lesser Hawkbit	Caisearbhan as Lugha
Lepidium campestre	Field Pepperwort	Lus a' Phiobair
Lepidium heterophyllum	Smith's Pepperwort	Piobar an Duine Bhochd
Leucanthemum vulgare	Oxeye Daisy	Neòinean Mòr/ *cairt wheel, horse gowan, (large) white gowan, dog daisy*
Leymus arenarius	Lyme-grass	Taithean
Ligusticum scoticum	Scots Lovage	Sunais
Ligustrum vulgare	Wild Privet	Ras-chrann Sìor-uaine
Limonium humile	Lax-flowered Sea-lavender	
Limonium recurvum	Rock Sea-lavender	
Limonium vulgare	Common Sea-lavender	
Limosella aquatica	Mudwort	Lus a' Phuill
Linaria repens	Pale Toadflax	Buabh-lìon Liath
Linaria vulgaris	Common Toadflax	Buabh-lìon Coitcheann
Linnaea borealis	Twinflower	Lus Linneuis

Latin	Common	Gaelic/Scots
Linum catharticum	Fairy Flax	Lìon nam Ban-sìdh
Linum perenne	Perennial Flax	
Listera cordata	Lesser Twayblade	Dà-dhuilleach Monaidh
Listera ovata	Common Twayblade	Dà-dhuilleach Coitcheann
Littorella uniflora	Shoreweed	Lus Bòrd an Locha
Lobelia dortmanna	Water Lobelia	Flùr an Lochain
Loiseleuria procumbens	Trailing Azalea	Lusan Albannach
Lolium perenne	Perennial Rye-grass	Feur-seagail, Breòillean
Lonicera periclymenum	Honeysuckle	Lus na Meala, Iadh-shlat/ *bin(d)wood, hinniesickle*
Lotus corniculatus	Common Bird's-foot-trefoil	Barra-mhìslean, Peasair a' Mhadaidh-ruadh/ *catcluke, craw tae(s)*
Lotus pedunculatus	Greater Bird's-foot-trefoil	Barra-mhìslean Lèana
Luzula arcuata	Curved Wood-rush	Learman Crom
Luzula campestris	Field Wood-rush	Learman Raoin
Luzula multiflora	Heath Wood-rush	Learman Monaidh
Luzula pilosa	Hairy Wood-rush	Learman Fionnach
Luzula spicata	Spiked Wood-rush	Learman Ailpeach
Luzula sylvatica	Great Wood-rush	Luachair Coille
Lychnis alpina	Alpine Catchfly	Coirean Ailpeach
Lychnis flos-cuculi	Ragged-Robin	Caorag Lèana, Sìoda-lus
Lychnis viscaria	Sticky Catchfly	Coirean Leantalach
Lycopodiella inundata	Marsh Clubmoss	Garbhag Lèana
Lycopodium annotinum	Interrupted Clubmoss	Lus a' Bhalgair
Lycopodium clavatum	Stag's-horn Clubmoss	Lus a' Mhadaidh-Ruaidh, Garbhag nan Gleann/ *fox fit, tod('s) tail(s)*
Lycopus europaeus	Gypsywort	Feòran Curraidh
Lysimachia nemorum	Yellow Pimpernel	Seamrag Moire
Lysimachia nummularia	Creeping-Jenny	Lus Cùinneach
Lysimachia thyrsiflora	Tufted Loosestrife	Conaire Dosach
Lysimachia vulgaris	Yellow Loosestrife	Seileachan Buidhe
Lythrum portula	Water-purslane	Flùr Bogaich Ealaidheach
Lythrum salicaria	Purple-loosestrife	Lus na Sìochaint

Latin	Common	Gaelic/Scots
Malus sylvestris	Crab Apple	Goirteag/*scrab, craw(s) aipple, scrog, crow(s) aipple*
Malva moschata	Musk-mallow	Ucas Fiadhain
Malva sylvestris	Common Mallow	Lus nam Meall Mòra/*maws*
Matricaria recutita	Scented Mayweed	Buidheag an Arbhair Chùbhraidh
Medicago lupulina	Black Medick	Dubh-mheidig
Melampyrum pratense	Common Cow-wheat	Càraid Bhuidhe
Melampyrum sylvaticum	Small Cow-wheat	Càraid Bhuidhe Bheag
Melica nutans	Mountain Melick	Meilig an t-Slèibhe Critheanach
Melica uniflora	Wood Melick	Meilig Coille
Mentha aquatica	Water Mint	Meannt an Uisge
Mentha arvensis	Corn Mint	Meannt an Arbhair/*lambs tongue*
Menyanthes trifoliata	Bogbean	Trì-bhileach/*threefold*
Mercurialis perennis	Dog's Mercury	Lus Glinne
Mertensia maritima	Oysterplant	Tìodhlac na Mara
Meum athamanticum	Spignel	Muilceann, Bricean Dubh/*micken, bad-money*
Milium effusum	Wood Millet	Mileid Choille
Minuartia rubella	Mountain Sandwort	Gaineamh-lus Artach
Minuartia sedoides	Cyphel	Lus an Tuim Chòinnich
Minuartia verna	Spring Sandwort	Gaineamh-lus an Earraich
Moehringia trinervia	Three-nerved Sandwort	Lus nan Naoi Alt Tri-fèitheach
Molinia caerulea	Purple Moor-grass	Fianach/*blaw grass, fly in bent, flee in bent*
Moneses uniflora	One-flowered Wintergreen	Glas-luibh Chùbhraidh
Monotropa hypopitys	Yellow Bird's-nest	
Montia fontana	Blinks	Fliodh Uisge
Mycelis muralis	Wall Lettuce	Bliotsan
Myosotis alpestris	Alpine Forget-me-not	Lus Midhe Ailpeach
Myosotis arvensis	Field Forget-me-not	Lus Midhe Aitich
Myosotis discolor	Changing Forget-me-not	Lus Midhe Caochlaideach
Myosotis laxa	Tufted Forget-me-not	Lus Midhe Dosach
Myosotis ramosissima	Early Forget-me-not	Lus Midhe Tràth
Myosotis scorpioides	Water Forget-me-not	Cotharach

Latin	Common	Gaelic/Scots
Myosotis secunda	Creeping Forget-me-not	Lus Midhe Ealaidheach
Myosotis stolonifera	Pale Forget-me-not	
Myosotis sylvatica	Wood Forget-me-not	Lus Midhe Coille
Myosoton aquaticum	Water Chickweed	Fliodh Uisge Mòr
Myrica gale	Bog-myrtle	Roid/*gall*
Myriophyllum alterniflorum	Alternate Water-milfoil	Snàthainn Bhàthaidh
Myriophyllum spicatum	Spiked Water-milfoil	Snàthainn Spìceach
Najas flexilis	Slender Naiad	Aibhneag
Nardus stricta	Mat-grass	Riasg
Narthecium ossifragum	Bog Asphodel	Bliochan
Neottia nidus-avis	Bird's-nest Orchid	Mogairlean Nead an Eòin
Nuphar lutea	Yellow Water-lily	Duilleag-bhàite Bhuidhe
Nuphar pumila	Least Water-lily	Duilleag-bhàite Bheag
Nymphaea alba	White Water-lily	Duilleag-bhàite Bhàn
Odontites vernus	Red Bartsia	Modhalan Coitcheann
Oenanthe aquatica	Fine-leaved Water-dropwort	Dàtha Bàn Uisge
Oenanthe crocata	Hemlock Water-dropwort	Dàtha Bàn Iteodha/*hech-how*
Oenanthe fistulosa	Tubular Water-dropwort	Dàtha Bàn Pìobach
Oenanthe lachenalii	Parsley Water-dropwort	Dàtha Bàn Peirsill
Ononis reclinata	Small Restharrow	
Ononis repens	Common Restharrow	Sreang Bogha
Ononis spinosa	Spiny Restharrow	Sreang Bogha Bhiorach
Ophioglossum azoricum	Small Adder's-tongue	Teanga na Nathrach Beag
Ophioglossum vulgatum	Adder's-tongue	Teanga na Nathrach
Orchis mascula	Early-purple Orchid	Moth-ùrach *bulls-bags*
Orchis morio	Green-winged Orchid	
Oreopteris limbosperma	Lemon-scented Fern	Crim-raineach, Raineach an Fhàile
Origanum vulgare	Wild Marjoram	Oragan, Lus Marsaili
Ornithopus perpusillus	Bird's-foot	Crubh Eòin

Latin	Common	Gaelic/Scots
Orobanche alba	Thyme Broomrape	Siorralach
Orobanche hederae	Ivy Broomrape	
Orobanche minor	Common Broomrape	
Orobanche rapum-genistae	Greater Broomrape	Siorralach Mòr
Orthilia secunda	Serrated Wintergreen	Glas-luibh Fhiaclach
Osmunda regalis	Royal Fern	Raineach Rìoghail
Oxalis acetosella	Wood-sorrel	Feada-coille, Biadh nan Eòinean/*gowk's meat, suckie sourocks, soukie sourocks*
Oxyria digyna	Mountain Sorrel	Sealbhag nam Fiadh
Oxytropis campestris	Yellow Oxytropis	Ogsatropas Buidhe
Oxytropis halleri	Purple Oxytropis	Ogsatropas Corcarach
Papaver dubium	Long-headed Poppy	Crom-lus Fad-cheannach
Papaver rhoeas	Common Poppy	Meilbheag/*puppie*
Parapholis strigosa	Hard-grass	Dùr-fheur Fairge
Parentucellia viscosa	Yellow Bartsia	
Parietaria judaica	Pellitory-of-the-wall	Lus a' Bhalla
Paris quadrifolia	Herb-paris	Aon-dhearc/*devil in a bush, deil in a bush*
Parnassia palustris	Grass-of-Parnassus	Fionnan Geal
Pedicularis palustris	Marsh Lousewort	Lus Riabhach
Pedicularis sylvatica	Lousewort	Lus Riabhach Monaidh, Lus/nam Mial
Persicaria amphibia	Amphibious Bistort	Glùineach an Uisge
Persicaria bistorta	Common Bistort	Biolur
Persicaria hydropiper	Water-pepper	Glùineach Theth
Persicaria lapathifolia	Pale Persicaria	Glùineach Bhàn
Persicaria maculosa	Redshank	Glùineach Dhearg
Persicaria minor	Small Water-pepper	
Persicaria vivipara	Alpine Bistort	Biolur Ailpeach
Petasites hybridus	Butterbur	Gallan Mòr/*gaun, paddock pipes, paddy pipes, son-afore-the-father, tushilago, puddock pipes, wild rhubarb*

Latin	Common	Gaelic/Scots
Phalaris arundinacea	Reed Canary-grass	Cuiseagrach
Phegopteris connectilis	Beech Fern	Raineach Fhaidhbhile
Phleum alpinum	Alpine Cat's-tail	Feur Cait Ailpeach
Phleum arenarium	Sand Cat's-tail	Feur Cait Gainmhich
Phleum bertolonii	Smaller Cat's-tail	Feur Cait Beag
Phleum pratense	Timothy	Feur Cait
Phragmites australis	Common Reed	Cuilc/*loch reed, risp (grass)*
Phyllitis scolopendrium	Hart's-tongue	Teanga an Fhèidh
Phyllodoce caerulea	Blue Heath	Fraoch a' Mhèinnearaich
Pilosella flagellaris	Shetland Mouse-ear-hawkweed	
Pilosella officinarum	Mouse-ear-hawkweed	Srubhan na Muice
Pilularia globulifera	Pillwort	Feur a' Phiobair
Pimpinella saxifraga	Burnet-saxifrage	Ainis Fhiadhain
Pinguicula alpina	Alpine Butterwort	
Pinguicula lusitanica	Pale Butterwort	Mòthan Beag Bàn
Pinguicula vulgaris	Common Butterwort	Mòthan
Pinus sylvestris	Scots Pine	Giuthas/*bonnet fir*
Plantago coronopus	Buck's-horn Plantain	Adhairc Fèidh
Plantago lanceolata	Ribwort Plantain	Slàn-lus/*curl-doddy, carl-doddie, ripple grass, hard heid(s)*
Plantago major	Greater Plantain	Cuach Phàdraig/*waverin leaf, leddy nit, curl-doddy, healin(g) blade, ripple grass, lady nit, tirlie-tod, wayburn leaf, rat('s)tail, healin(g) leaf, carl-doddie, warba (blade)*
Plantago maritima	Sea Plantain	Slàn-lus na Mara
Plantago media	Hoary Plantain	Slàn-lus Liath/*lambs ears, lamb's lugs*
Platanthera bifolia	Lesser Butterfly-orchid	Mogairlean an Dealain-dè Beag
Platanthera chlorantha	Greater Butterfly-orchid	Mogairlean an Dealain-dè Mòr
Poa alpina	Alpine Meadow-grass	Tràthach Ailpeach
Poa angustifolia	Narrow-leaved Meadow-grass	Tràthach na Duilleige Caoile
Poa annua	Annual Meadow-grass	Tràthach Bliadhnail
Poa compressa	Flattened Meadow-grass	Tràthach Teannaichte
Poa flexuosa	Wavy Meadow-grass	Tràthach Casta

Latin	Common	Gaelic/Scots
Poa glauca	Glaucous Meadow-grass	Tràthach Liath-ghorm
Poa humilis	Spreading Meadow-grass	Tràthach Sgaoilte
Poa nemoralis	Wood Meadow-grass	Tràthach Coille
Poa pratensis	Smooth Meadow-grass	Tràthach Mìn
Poa trivialis	Rough Meadow-grass	Tràthach Garbh
Polygala serpyllifolia	Heath Milkwort	Siabann nam Ban-sìdh
Polygala vulgaris	Common Milkwort	Lus a' Bhainne
Polygonatum odoratum	Angular Solomon's-seal	
Polygonatum verticillatum	Whorled Solomon's-seal	
Polygonum arenastrum	Equal-leaved Knotgrass	Glùineach Ghainmhich
Polygonum aviculare	Knotgrass	Glùineach Bheag/*feenich, midden weed*
Polygonum boreale	Northern Knotgrass	Glùineach Thuathach
Polygonum oxyspermum	Ray's Knotgrass	Glùineach na Tràighe
Polygonum rurivagum	Cornfield Knotgrass	
Polypodium cambricum	Southern Polypody	Clach-raineach Leathann
Polypodium interjectum	Intermediate Polypody	Clach-raineach Mheadhanach
Polypodium vulgare	Polypody	Clach-raineach Chaol/*ernfern*
Polystichum aculeatum	Hard Shield-fern	Ibhig Chruaidh
Polystichum lonchitis	Holly-fern	Raineach Chuilinn
Polystichum setiferum	Soft Shield-fern	Ibhig Bhog
Populus tremula	Aspen	Critheann/*esp, tremmlin tree, quakin a(i)sh, quakin trei, quakin asp*
Potamogeton alpinus	Red Pondweed	Lìobhag Dhearg
Potamogeton berchtoldii	Small Pondweed	Lìobhag Bheag
Potamogeton coloratus	Fen Pondweed	Lìobhag Rèisg
Potamogeton compressus	Grass-wrack Pondweed	
Potamogeton crispus	Curled Pondweed	Lìobhag Chamagach
Potamogeton epihydrus	American Pondweed	Lìobhag Aimeireaganach
Potamogeton filiformis	Slender-leaved Pondweed	Lìobhag Chaol
Potamogeton friesii	Flat-stalked Pondweed	Lìobhag Reiteach
Potamogeton gramineus	Various-leaved Pondweed	Lìobhag Fheurach
Potamogeton lucens	Shining Pondweed	Lìobhag Loinnreach
Potamogeton natans	Broad-leaved Pondweed	Duileasg na h-Aibhne
Potamogeton obtusifolius	Blunt-leaved Pondweed	Lìobhag Mhaol
Potamogeton pectinatus	Fennel Pondweed	Lìobhag Fhineil

Latin	Common	Gaelic/Scots
Potamogeton perfoliatus	Perfoliate Pondweed	Dreimire Uisge
Potamogeton polygonifolius	Bog Pondweed	Lìobhag Bogaich
Potamogeton praelongus	Long-stalked Pondweed	Lìobhag Fhada
Potamogeton pusillus	Lesser Pondweed	Lìobhag Mhion
Potamogeton rutilus	Shetland Pondweed	Lìobhag Ruadh
Potamogeton trichoides	Hairlike Pondweed	
Potentilla anglica	Trailing Tormentil	Cairt Làir Ealaidheach
Potentilla anserina	Silverweed	Brisgean/*mascorn*
Potentilla argentea	Hoary Cinquefoil	Cairt Làir Liath
Potentilla crantzii	Alpine Cinquefoil	Leamhnach Ailpeach
Potentilla erecta	Tormentil	Cairt Làir, Leamhnach
Potentilla neumanniana	Spring Cinquefoil	Leamhnach an Earraich
Potentilla palustris	Marsh Cinquefoil	Còig-bhileach Uisge
Potentilla reptans	Creeping Cinquefoil	Còig-bhileach
Potentilla rupestris	Rock Cinquefoil	
Potentilla sterilis	Barren Strawberry	Sùbh-làir Brèige
Primula scotica	Scottish Primrose	Sòbhrach Albannach
Primula veris	Cowslip	Muisean/*lady's fingers, ladies' fingers*
Primula vulgaris	Primrose	Sòbhrach/*maisie spink, buckie-faulie, spink, plumrose, pinkie, meysie spink*
Prunella vulgaris	Selfheal	Dubhan Ceann-chòsach/*puir man's clover, crochle girs, hert of the yearth*
Prunus avium	Wild Cherry	Geanais/*gean*
Prunus padus	Bird Cherry	Fiodhag/*hawkberry, hagberry*
Prunus spinosa	Blackthorn	Preas nan Airneag/*slae*
Pseudorchis albida	Small-white Orchid	Mogairlean Bàn Beag
Pteridium aquilinum	Bracken	Raineach Mhòr/*fern, brachan, rannoch, brechan*
Puccinellia distans	Reflexed Saltmarsh-grass	
Puccinellia maritima	Common Saltmarsh-grass	Feur Rèisg Ghoirt
Pulicaria dysenterica	Common Fleabane	Fuath-dheargann
Pyrola media	Intermediate Wintergreen	Glas-luibh Meadhanach
Pyrola minor	Common Wintergreen	Glas-luibh Beag
Pyrola rotundifolia	Round-leaved Wintergreen	Glas-luibh Cruinn

Latin	Common	Gaelic/Scots
Quercus petraea	Sessile Oak	Darach/*aik*
Quercus robur	Pedunculate Oak	Darach Gasagach
Radiola linoides	Allseed	Lus Meanbh Meanganach
Ranunculus acris	Meadow Buttercup	Buidheag an t Samhraidh/*crow-tae(s), craw-tae(s)*
Ranunculus aquatilis	Common Water-crowfoot	Fleann Uisge
Ranunculus arvensis	Corn Buttercup	
Ranunculus auricomus	Goldilocks Buttercup	Gruag Moire/*goldilocks*
Ranunculus baudotii	Brackish Water-crowfoot	Fleann Uisge Shaillte
Ranunculus bulbosus	Bulbous Buttercup	Fuile-thalmhainn
Ranunculus circinatus	Fan-leaved Water-crowfoot	Fleann Uisge Rag
Ranunculus ficaria	Lesser Celandine	Searragaich, Gràn Aigein
Ranunculus flammula	Lesser Spearwort	Glaisleun/*wild fire*
Ranunculus fluitans	River Water-crowfoot	Fleann Uisge Aibhne
Ranunculus hederaceus	Ivy-leaved Crowfoot	Fleann Uisge Eidheannach
Ranunculus lingua	Greater Spearwort	Glaisleun Mòr
Ranunculus omiophyllus	Round-leaved Crowfoot	Fleann Uisge Chruinn
Ranunculus peltatus	Pond Water-crowfoot	Fleann Uisge Linne
Ranunculus penicillatus	Stream Water-crowfoot	
Ranunculus repens	Creeping Buttercup	Buidheag/*hen taes, fox-fit, crow-tae(s), craw-tae(s)*
Ranunculus reptans	Creeping Spearwort	Glaisleun Ealaidheach
Ranunculus sardous	Hairy Buttercup	Buidheag Fhionnach
Ranunculus sceleratus	Celery-leaved Buttercup	Torachas Biadhain
Ranunculus trichophyllus	Thread-leaved Water-crowfoot	Lìon na h-Aibhne
Raphanus raphanistrum	Wild Radish	Meacan Ruadh Fiadhain/*runchick, runchie, wild kail, reefort minnonette*
Reseda lutea	Wild Mignonette	
Reseda luteola	Weld	Lus Buidhe Mòr/*straw wald, strae wald, wald*
Rhinanthus angustifolius	Greater Yellow-rattle	
Rhinanthus minor	Yellow-rattle	Modhalan Buidhe
Rhynchospora alba	White Beak-sedge	Gob-sheisg
Rhynchospora fusca	Brown Beak-sedge	Gob-sheisg Ruadh

Latin	Common	Gaelic/Scots
Ribes nigrum	Black Currant	Dearc Dhubh/ *blackberry, black russle, black rizzar*
Ribes spicatum	Downy Currant	
Ribes uva-crispa	Gooseberry	Gròiseid/ *honey blob, blob, grosart, hinnie-blob, greenberry, groser, groset, grosell*
Rorippa amphibia	Great Yellow-crest	
Rorippa islandica	Northern Yellow-cress	Biolair Bhuidhe Thuathach
Rorippa microphylla	Narrow-fruited Water-cress	Mion-bhiolair
Rorippa nasturtium-aquaticum	Water-cress	Biolair Uisge/ *wall grass, wall kerse, well kerse, wall girse kail, carse(s), well girse kail, well grass*
Rorippa palustris	Marsh Yellow-cress	
Rorippa sylvestris	Creeping Yellow-cress	Biolair Bhuidhe Ealaidheach
Rosa caesia	Hairy Dog-rose	
Rosa canina	Dog-rose	Ròs nan Con
Rosa micrantha	Small-flowered Sweet-briar	
Rosa mollis	Soft Downy-rose	Ròs Bog
Rosa pimpinellifolia	Burnet Rose	Ròs Beag Bàn na h-Alba, Dreas nam Mucag
Rosa rubiginosa	Sweet-briar	Dris Chùbhraidh
Rosa sherardii	Sherard's Downy-rose	Ròs Shioraird
Rosa tomentosa	Harsh Downy-rose	
Rubus articus	Arctic Bramble	
Rubus caesius	Dewberry	Preas nan Gorm-dhearc
Rubus chamaemorus	Cloudberry	Lus nan Oighreag/ *noop, knot(berry), averin*
Rubus fruticosus	Bramble	Dris/ *black byde, lady('s) garters, lady('s) gairtens, bramble, ladies' garter(s), brammle, ladies' gartens*
Rubus idaeus	Raspberry	Sùbh-craoibh/ *thimbles, himberry, thummles, hindberry, siven*
Rubus saxatilis	Stone Bramble	Caor Bad Miann
Rumex acetosa	Common Sorrel	Samh, Sealbhag/ *rantie-tantie, rid-shank, sourock dock(en), redshank, sourock leek, reid-shank*

93

Latin	Common	Gaelic/Scots
Rumex acetosella	Sheep's Sorrel	Sealbhag nan Caorach/*lammie sourocks*
Rumex aquaticus	Scottish Dock	Copag Albannach
Rumex conglomeratus	Clustered Dock	Copag Bhagaideach
Rumex crispus	Curled Dock	Copag Chamagach/*docken*
Rumex hydrolapathum	Water Dock	Copag Uisge
Rumex longifolius	Northern Dock	Copag Thuathach
Rumex maritimus	Golden Dock	
Rumex obtusifolius	Broad-leaved Dock	Copag Leathann/*docken, reid-shank, docken, rìd-shank, red-shank*
Rumex sanguineus	Blood-veined Dock	
Ruppia cirrhosa	Spiral Tasselweed	Snàth-lus Camagach
Ruppia maritima	Beaked Tasselweed	
Sagina apetala	Annual Pearlwort	Mungan
Sagina maritima	Sea Pearlwort	Mungan Mara
Sagina nivalis	Snow Pearlwort	
Sagina nodosa	Knotted Pearlwort	Mungan Snaimte
Sagina procumbens	Procumbent Pearlwort	Mungan Làir
Sagina saginoides	Alpine Pearlwort	Mungan Ailpeach
Sagina subulata	Heath Pearlwort	Mungan Mòintich
Salicornia dolichostachya	Long-spiked Glasswort	
Salicornia europaea	Common Glasswort	Lus na Glainne
Salicornia fragilis	Yellow Glasswort	
Salicornia nitens	Shiny Glasswort	
Salicornia ramosissima	Purple Glasswort	
Salix alba	White Willow	Seileach Bàn
Salix arbuscula	Mountain Willow	Seileach an t-Slèibhe
Salix aurita	Eared Willow	Seileach Cluasach
Salix caprea	Goat Willow	Geal-sheileach, Sùileag/*palm (tree), sauch willie*
Salix cinerea	Grey Willow	
Salix fragilis	Crack-willow	Seileach Brisg
Salix herbacea	Dwarf Willow	Seileach Ailpeach
Salix lanata	Woolly Willow	Seileach Clòimheach

94

Latin	Common	Gaelic/Scots
Salix lapponum	Downy Willow	Seileach Clùimhteach
Salix myrsinifolia	Dark-leaved Willow	Seileach na Duilleige Duirche
Salix myrsinites	Whortle-leaved Willow	Seileach Miortail
Salix pentandra	Bay Willow	Seileach Labhrais
Salix phylicifolia	Tea-leaved Willow	Seileach Tuathach
Salix purpurea	Purple Willow	Seileach Corcarach
Salix repens	Creeping Willow	Seileach Làir
Salix reticulata	Net-leaved Willow	Seileach Lìonanach
Salix viminalis	Osier	Seileach Uisge/*osare*
Salsola kali	Prickly Saltwort	
Salvia verbenaca	Wild Clary	Torman
Sambucus nigra	Elder	Droman/*bourtree, eller, bountree*
Samolus valerandi	Brookweed	Luibh an t-Sruthain
Sanguisorba minor	Salad Burnet	A' Bhileach Losgainn
Sanguisorba officinalis	Great Burnet	A' Bhileach Losgainn Mhòr
Sanicula europaea	Sanicle	Bodan Coille
Saussurea alpina	Alpine Saw-wort	Sàbh-lus Ailpeach
Saxifraga aizoides	Yellow Saxifrage	Clach-bhriseach Bhuidhe
Saxifraga cernua	Drooping Saxifrage	Lus Bheinn Labhair
Saxifraga cespitosa	Tufted Saxifrage	Clach-bhriseach Dhosach
Saxifraga granulata	Meadow Saxifrage	Moran
Saxifraga hirculus	Marsh Saxifrage	Moran Rèisg
Saxifraga hypnoides	Mossy Saxifrage	Clach-bhriseach Còinnich
Saxifraga nivalis	Alpine Saxifrage	Clach-bhriseach an t-Sneachda
Saxifraga oppositifolia	Purple Saxifrage	Clach-bhriseach Phurpaidh
Saxifraga rivularis	Highland Saxifrage	Clach-bhriseach an t-Slèibhe
Saxifraga stellaris	Starry Saxifrage	Clach-bhriseach Reultach
Saxifraga tridactylites	Rue-leaved Saxifrage	Clach-bhriseach na Machrach
Scabiosa columbaria	Small Scabious	
Scandix pecten-veneris	Shepherd's-needle	
Scheuchzeria palustris	Rannoch-rush	Luachair Rainich
Schoenoplectus lacustris	Common Club-rush	Luachair Ghòbhlach
Schoenoplectus tabernaemontani	Grey Club-rush	Luachair Bhogain
Schoenus ferrugineus	Brown Bog-rush	Sèimhean Ruadh
Schoenus nigricans	Black Bog-rush	Sèimhean Dubh
Scilla verna	Spring Squill	Lear-uinnean
Scirpus sylvaticus	Wood Club-rush	Bròbh Coille

Latin	Common	Gaelic/Scots
Scleranthus annuus	Annual Knawel	
Scrophularia auriculata	Water Figwort	Lus nan Cnapan Uisge
Scrophularia nodosa	Common Figwort	Lus nan Cnapan
Scrophularia umbrosa	Green Figwort	
Scutellaria galericulata	Skullcap	Cochall
Scutellaria minor	Lesser Skullcap	Cochall Beag
Sedum acre	Biting Stonecrop	Gràbhan nan Clach
Sedum anglicum	English Stonecrop	Biadh an t-Sionnaidh
Sedum rosea	Roseroot	Lus nan Laoch
Sedum telephium	Orpine	Orp/*orpie, wurpie*
Sedum villosum	Hairy Stonecrop	Gràbhan nan Clach Giobach
Selaginella selaginoides	Lesser Clubmoss	Garbhag Bheag
Senecio aquaticus	Marsh Ragwort	Caoibhreachan
Senecio cambrensis	Welsh Groundsel	
Senecio erucifolius	Hoary Ragwort	
Senecio jacobaea	Common Ragwort	Buaghallan/*bowlocks, benweed, ragweed, bunweed, weebie(s), stinking Elshender, stinkin Willie, tansy*
Senecio sylvaticus	Heath Groundsel	Grunnasg Monaidh
Senecio viscosus	Sticky Groundsel	Grunnasg Leantalach
Senecio vulgaris	Groundsel	Grunnasg/*grundiswallow*
Seriphidium maritimum	Sea Wormwood	
Serratula tinctoria	Saw-wort	
Sesleria caerulea	Blue Moor-grass	
Sherardia arvensis	Field Madder	Màdar na Machrach
Sibbaldia procumbens	Sibbaldia	Siobaldag
Silaum silaus	Pepper-saxifrage	
Silene acaulis	Moss Campion	Coirean Còinnich
Silene conica	Sand Catchfly	Coirean Gainmhich
Silene dioica	Red Campion	Cìrean Coilich
Silene gallica	Small-flowered Catchfly	
Silene latifolia	White Campion	Coirean Bàn
Silene noctiflora	Night-flowering Catchfly	
Silene nutans	Nottingham Catchfly	
Silene uniflora	Sea Campion	Coirean na Mara
Silene vulgaris	Bladder Campion	Coirean nam Balgan/*coo-cracker*

Latin	Common	Gaelic/Scots
Sinapis arvensis	Charlock	Sgeallan/*skellie(s), skelloch(s), scaldrick, skeldock, wild kail*
Sisymbrium officinale	Hedge Mustard	Meilise
Sium latifolium	Greater Water-parsnip	Folachdan Mòr
Solanum dulcamara	Bittersweet	Searbhag Mhilis, Fuath Gorm/*pushion berry*
Solidago virgaurea	Goldenrod	Slat Oir
Sonchus arvensis	Perennial Sow-thistle	Bliochd Fochainn
Sonchus asper	Prickly Sow-thistle	Searbhan Muice
Sonchus oleraceus	Smooth Sow-thistle	Bainne Muice/*swine('s) th(r)issle, rabbit thissle*
Sorbus aria	Common Whitebeam	Gall-uinnsean/*mulberry*
Sorbus arranensis	Whitebeam	
Sorbus aucuparia	Rowan	Caorann/*rowan buss, rone-tree, rone buss, rowan-tree, rodden-tree, rodden*
Sorbus pseudofennica	Arran Service-tree	
Sorbus rupicola	Rock Whitebeam	Gall-uinnsean na Creige
Sparganium angustifolium	Floating Bur-reed	Seisg Rìgh air Bhog
Sparganium emersum	Unbranched Bur-reed	Seisg Rìgh Madaidh
Sparganium erectum	Branched Bur-reed	Seisg Rìgh
Sparganium natans	Least Bur-reed	Seisg Rìgh Mion
Spergula arvensis	Corn Spurrey	Cluain-lìn, Corran-lìn/*yarr*
Spergularia marina	Lesser Sea-spurrey	Corran Mara Beag
Spergularia media	Greater Sea-spurrey	Corran Mara Mòr
Spergularia rubra	Sand Spurrey	Corran Gainmhich
Spergularia rupicola	Rock Sea-spurrey	Corran na Creige
Spiranthes romanzoffiana	Irish Lady's-tresses	Mogairlean Bachlach Bàn
Stachys arvensis	Field Woundwort	Creuchd-lus Arbhair
Stachys officinalis	Betony	Lus Beathaig
Stachys palustris	Marsh Woundwort	Brisgean nan Caorach
Stachys sylvatica	Hedge Woundwort	Lus nan Sgor
Stellaria graminea	Lesser Stitchwort	Tursarain
Stellaria holostea	Greater Stitchwort	Tursach
Stellaria media	Common Chickweed	Fliodh/*chickenwort, chickenweed*
Stellaria neglecta	Greater Chickweed	Fliodh Mhòr
Stellaria nemorum	Wood Stitchwort	Tursarain Choille

Latin	Common	Gaelic/Scots
Stellaria pallida	Lesser Chickweed	Fliodh Bheag
Stellaria palustris	Marsh Stitchwort	Tursarain Lèana
Stellaria uliginosa	Bog Stitchwort	Flige
Suaeda maritima	Annual Sea-blite	Praiseach na Mara
Subularia aquatica	Awlwort	Lus a' Mhinidh
Succisa pratensis	Devil's-bit Scabious	Ura-bhallach/ *bluebonnets, curl-doddy*
Symphytum officinale	Common Comfrey	Meacan Dubh
Symphytum tuberosum	Tuberous Comfrey	Meacan Dubh Cnapach
Tanacetum vulgare	Tansy	Lus na Fhainge/ *stinkin Tam(my)*
Taraxacum officinale	Dandelion	Beàrnan Brìde/ *methick, pish-the-bed, horse gowan, pee-the-bed, dent-de-lyon, dainty-lion, medick, what o'clock is it?*
Taxus baccata	Yew	Iubhar
Teesdalia nudicaulis	Shepherd's Cress	Biolair a' Bhuachaille
Teucrium scorodonia	Wood Sage	Sàisde Coille
Thalictrum alpinum	Alpine Meadow-rue	Rù Ailpeach
Thalictrum flavum	Common Meadow-rue	
Thalictrum minus	Lesser Meadow-rue	Rù Beag
Thelypteris palustris	Marsh Fern	Raineach Lèana
Thlaspi arvense	Field Penny-cress	Praiseach Fèidh
Thlaspi caerulescens	Alpine Penny-cress	
Thymus polytrichus	Wild Garden Thyme	Lus an Rìgh, Lus na Macraidh
Thymus pulegioides	Large Garden Thyme	
Tofieldia pusilla	Scottish Asphodel	Bliochan Albannach
Torilis japonica	Upright Hedge-parsley	Peirsill Fàil
Torilis nodosa	Knotted Hedge-parsley	
Tragopogon pratensis	Goat's-beard	Feusag a' Ghobhair
Trichomanes speciosum	Killarney Fern	Raineach Chill Airne
Trichophorum alpinum	Cotton Deergrass	
Trichophorum cespitosum	Deergrass	Cìob, Ultanaich/ *ling, deer('s) hair*

Latin	Common	Gaelic/Scots
Trientalis europaea	Chickweed-wintergreen	Reul na Coille
Trifolium arvense	Hare's-foot Clover	Cas Maighiche
Trifolium campestre	Hop Trefoil	Seamrag Bhuidhe
Trifolium dubium	Lesser Trefoil	Seangan
Trifolium fragiferum	Strawberry Clover	
Trifolium medium	Zigzag Clover	Seamrag Chrò-dhearg
Trifolium micranthum	Slender Trefoil	
Trifolium ornithopodioides	Bird's-foot Clover	Crubh-eòin
Trifolium pratense	Red Clover	Seamrag Dhearg
Trifolium repens	White Clover	Seamrag Bhàn/*white sookie(s)*
Trifolium scabrum	Rough Clover	
Trifolium striatum	Knotted Clover	
Triglochin maritimum	Sea Arrowgrass	Barr a' Mhilltich Mara
Triglochin palustre	Marsh Arrowgrass	Barr a' Mhilltich Lèana
Tripleurospermum inodorum	Scentless Mayweed	Buidheag an Arbhair
Tripleurospermum maritimum	Sea Mayweed	Buidheag na Mara
Trisetum flavescens	Yellow Oat-grass	Feur Coirce Buidhe
Trollius europaeus	Globeflower	Leolaicheann/*lapper gowan, lucken gowan, butter blob*
Tussilago farfara	Colt's-foot	Cluas Liath/*doo-docken, tushilago, son-afore-the-father, shilagie*
Typha angustifolia	Lesser Bulrush	Bodan
Typha latifolia	Bulrush	Cuigeal nam Ban-sìdh
Ulex europaeus	Gorse	Conasg/*whun, whin*
Ulex gallii	Western Gorse	Conasg Siarach
Ulex minor	Dwarf Gorse	Conasg Mion
Ulmus glabra	Wych Elm	Leamhan
Umbilicus rupestris	Navelwort	Leacan/*maid in the mist*
Urtica dioica	Common Nettle	Deanntag, Feanntag/*Jinny nettle(s), Jenny nettle(s), jobbie nettle*
Urtica urens	Small Nettle	Deanntag Bhliadhnail
Utricularia australis	Bladderwort	Lus nam Balgan

Latin	Common	Gaelic/Scots
Utricularia intermedia	Intermediate Bladderwort	Lus nam Balgan Meadhanach
Utricularia minor	Lesser Bladderwort	Lus nam Balgan Beag
Utricularia ochroleuca	Pale Bladderwort	
Utricularia stygia	Nordic Bladderwort	
Utricularia vulgaris	Greater Bladderwort	Lus nam Balgan Mòr
Vaccinium microcarpum	Small Cranberry	
Vaccinium myrtillus	Bilberry	Caora-mhitheag/*blivert, blairdie, blaeberry*
Vaccinium oxycoccos	Cranberry	Muileag/*crawcrooks, crane, moss mingin*
Vaccinium uliginosum	Bog Bilberry	Dearc Roide
Vaccinium vitis-idaea	Cowberry	Lus nam Braoileag
Valeriana dioica	Marsh Valerian	Caoirin Lèana
Valeriana officinalis	Common Valerian	Carthan Curaidh/*valairie*
Valerianella dentata	Narrow-fruited Cornsalad	Leiteis an Uain Chaol
Valerianella locusta	Common Cornsalad	Leiteis an Uain
Valerianella rimosa	Broad-fruited Cornsalad	
Verbascum thapsus	Great Mullein Coinneal Moire	shepherd's club
Veronica agrestis	Green Field-speedwell	Lus-crè Arbhair
Veronica alpina	Alpine Speedwell	Lus-crè Ailpeach
Veronica anagallis-aquatica	Blue Water-Speedwell	Fualachdar
Veronica arvensis	Wall Speedwell	Lus-crè Balla
Veronica beccabunga	Brooklime	Lochal Mothair/*wellink, wallink, water purpie*
Veronica catenata	Pink Water-Speedwell	Lus-crè Uisge
Veronica chamaedrys	Germander Speedwell	An-uallach/*blawort, cat's een, blaver*
Veronica fruticans	Rock Speedwell	Lus-crè na Creige
Veronica hederifolia	Ivy-leaved Speedwell	Lus-crè Eidheannach
Veronica montana	Wood Speedwell	Lus-crè Coille
Veronica officinalis	Heath Speedwell	Lus-crè Monaidh/*Jenny's blue een, Jinny's blue een*
Veronica polita	Grey Field-speedwell	Lus-crè Liath
Veronica scutellata	Marsh Speedwell	Lus-crè Lèana

Latin	Common	Gaelic/Scots
Veronica serpyllifolia	Thyme-leaved Speedwell	Lus-crè Talmhainn
Viburnum opulus	Guelder-rose	Caor-chon/*veyton*
Vicia bithynica	Bithynian Vetch	
Vicia cracca	Tufted Vetch	Peasair nan Luch
Vicia hirsuta	Hairy Tare	Peasair an Arbhair/*teer*
Vicia lathyroides	Spring Vetch	Peasair an Earraich
Vicia lutea	Yellow-vetch	
Vicia orobus	Wood Bitter-vetch	Peasair Shearbh
Vicia sativa	Common Vetchhorse-peas(s)	
Vicia sepium	Bush Vetch	Peasair nam Preas
Vicia sylvatica	Wood Vetch	Peasair Coille
Vicia tetrasperma	Smooth Tare	
Viola arvensis	Field Pansy	Luibh Cridhe
Viola canina	Heath Dog-violet	Sàil-chuach
Viola hirta	Hairy Violet	Sàil-chuach Ghiobach
Viola lutea	Mountain Pansy	Sàil-chuach an t-Slèibhe
Viola palustris	Marsh Violet	Dail-chuach Lèana
Viola reichenbachiana	Early Dog-violet	Dail-chuach Tràth
Viola riviniana	Common Dog-violet	Dail-chuach
Viola tricolor	Wild Pansy	
Vulpia bromoides	Squirreltail Fescue	Feisd Aimrid
Vulpia fasciculata	Dune Fescue	
Vulpia myuros	Rat's-tail Fescue	
Wahlenbergia hederacea	Ivy-leaved Bellflower	
Woodsia alpina	Alpine Woodsia	Raineach Mhion Ailpeach
Woodsia ilvensis	Oblong Woodsia	Raineach Mhion Fhad-shliosach
Zannichellia palustris	Horned Pondweed	Lìobhag Adhairceach
Zostera angustifolia	Narrow-leaved Eelgrass	Bilearach na Duilleige Caoile
Zostera marina	Eelgrass	Bilearach
Zostera noltii	Dwarf Eelgrass	Bilearach Mion

INDEX